DULWICH AND CAMBERWELL PAST

First published 1997
by Historical Publications Ltd
32 Ellington Street, London N7 8PL
(Tel: 0171-607 1628)

ISBN 0 948667 44 3
British Library Cataloguing-in Publication Data
A catalogue record for this book is available from the British Library

Typeset in Palatino by Historical Publications Ltd
Reproduction by G & J Graphics, London EC2
Printed by Edelvives, Zaragoza, Spain

The Illustrations

We are grateful to the following for kindly supplying the illustrations:
Associated Press: *155*
The late Felix Barker: *143*
The Bishopsgate Institute: *34*
Tim Charlesworth: *153*
Roger Cline: *4, 97, 108, 159, 160*
Huntington Art Gallery, Pasadena, USA: *81*
London Borough of Lambeth: *106*
National Portrait Gallery: *57*
Newart Photographic: *154*
S & G Photographic Library: *156*
Richard Tames: *3, 16, 17, 29, 35, 36, 40, 51, 55, 61, 62, 63, 65, 73, 75, 77, 79, 85, 86, 88, 89, 93,
94, 112, 113, 116, 120, 128, 129, 130, 133, 134, 136, 137, 141, 147, 152, 157, 158*
Douglas Smith: *frontis, 90*
London Borough of Southwark: *1, 12, 13, 15, 28, 31, 37, 45, 46, 47, 58, 60, 64, 82, 83, 90, 98, 100,
102, 103, 104, 107, 109, 110, 114, 115, 117, 119, 124, 131, 132, 139, 145, 146, 148, 149, 150,
161, 163*
Wellcome Institute of Medicine: *49*
All other illustrations were supplied by Historical Publications Ltd

Historical Publications Ltd specialises in local history publishing.
A full list of our publications may be obtained on application to our distributors,
Phillimore & Co., Shopwyke Manor Barn, Chichester, Sussex PO20 6BG.

The publishers would be happy to receive proposals for other titles in this series.

DULWICH AND CAMBERWELL PAST

with Peckham

by Richard Tames

HISTORICAL PUBLICATIONS

The loading bay for horse-drawn distribution of Jones & Higgins in Peckham, early this century.

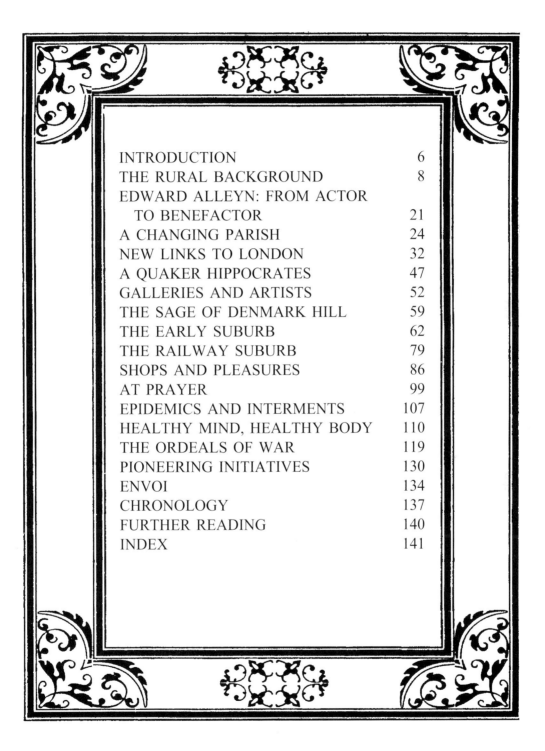

Introduction

" ... pleasantly retired, having no high road passing through it."
Priscilla Wakefield *Perambulations in London* (1809)

Dulwich is now synonymous with its famous Picture Gallery and College, which both owe their origins, albeit somewhat indirectly, to the charitable foundation of Shakespeare's theatrical contemporary, Edward Alleyn. Camberwell is currently described – or perhaps one should say dismissed – by a leading London guide book as "a busy but neglected part of London."

Peckham is where, in June 1997, Prime Minister Blair chose to make his first major post-election speech, on the relationship between welfare and the workless. Nunhead is, perhaps, best known for its cemetery, a pioneering venture in its day. Physically these areas are contiguous. Socially they are, at the least, quite distinctively different from one another.

Once they were all just parts of the ancient parish of Camberwell. In names their origins are betrayed. Dulwich was a meadow noted for its dill plants, Peckham in Old English 'the village by a hill', Nunhead the location of a nunnery. Of Camberwell the historian and local vicar, Lysons, noted in 1811 with caution and a hint of irritation: "I can find nothing satisfactory with respect to its etymology; the termination seems to point to some remarkable spring." That the suffix 'well' should denote a source of water seems, indeed, a reasonable speculation. But why remarkable? Perhaps because the prefatory particle 'cam' can denote 'crooked' or 'crippled' – hence implying healing prperties. This speculation is strengthened by the dedication of the ancient parish church to St Giles, patron saint of cripples, lepers and beggars.

The sylvan character of Camberwell's past is attested by the remarkable number of local streets styled 'Grove' and 'Dale' – and even more forcefully by the fact that it has given its name to a brilliant butterfly and that Mendelssohn's *Spring Song*, composed while he was visiting the area, was originally called *Camberwell Green*. For centuries the area enjoyed a reputation for unusual salubriousness, thereby favouring the construction of numerous gentlemen's residences, almshouses, asylums, hospitals, schools and hotels for which a healthy setting was an important consideration. In the eighteenth century it was not uncommon to refer to the locality as a spa. Pioneering local historian D.H.Allport meticulously recorded, a century after the event, the origins of this now seemingly unlikely aspect of the local heritage: "In the autumn of 1739 Mr Cox, the master of a well known house of good entertainment, called the Green Man at Dulwich ... was desirous to dig a well for the service of his house ... The well being digged to the depth of sixty feet, and no water appearing, Mr Cox caused it to be covered up, and gave himself no further trouble about it that winter." When the well was re-examined the following spring, however, it was found to contain "twenty-five feet of water of a sulphureous smell and taste." Professor John Martyn F.R.S. then subjected the water to an imaginatively broad range of tests and found that it curdled milk "... effervesced considerably with oils of vitriol and tartar ... did not lather soap ... and tarnished silver". Perhaps unsurprisingly, after demonstrating such effects, the Professor pronounced the water to constitute "a brisk purgative and diuretic" – which seems to have been endorsement enough for the enterprising Mr Cox not only to capitalise on it as an adjunct of the Green Man but also to sell it to St Bartholomew's Hospital in the City. His name lives on in Cox's Walk. The site of the Green Man later housed Dr Glennie's Academy, where Byron was a pupil, and later Old Bew's beerhouse and tea-gardens, which was eventually rebuilt as the Grove Tavern.

The transition of the four areas named above from their past to their present condition is the theme of this book. The arrangement of the chapters is broadly chronological, but the treatment is thematic rather than strictly narrative. Comprehensiveness is not to be achieved in so concise a compass as the format of this book. I am all too conscious, therefore, of its omissions, although comforted a little by the fact that such important aspects of the subject as the history of the area's distinguished schools has been thoroughly chronicled elsewhere.

But at every turn there are physical reminders of layers of history left untouched. Take the junction of Denmark Hill and Coldharbour Lane, where the Foyer centre now stands. For half a century it was the site of an Odeon cinema, before that of a music hall and theatre, before that of a grammar school and before that a gentleman's residence. I have therefore tried at points to resurrect the memory of some places now quite vanished, such as the fine French garden of Sir Thomas Bond and the influential nursery of plantsman Peter Collinson.

The past is about people as well as places. Again, I have focused on some individuals rather than others. I have given a whole chapter to Ruskin because Camberwell and Dulwich provided not only the crucible of his thought but also the context of most of his adult life, whereas Robert Browning, the most famous person actually to have been born in the area, moved away from it as an adult and was, arguably, far more influenced by, say, his relationship with Italy, than by his birthplace. And just as I have tried to give Collinson his due, so I have also decided to pay tribute to the remarkable Dr. Lettsom (p47) – which has meant omitting a number of distinguished residents whose major triumphs were achieved elsewhere. These include scientist Sir Henry Bessemer, Sir Hiram Maxim, inventor of the machine-gun, Mr Eno (he of the fruit salts), 'Mr. Bovril" (really Johnstone) and Elizabeth Cadbury (née Taylor), creator of the model estate at Bourneville, Birmingham. On the same grounds I have excluded the stories of such celebrated 'O.As' as the philosopher G.E. Moore, designer C.F.A. Voysey, scientist Sidney Gilchrist Thomas, explorer Sir Ernest Shackleton and writers C.S. Forester, Raymond Chandler and P.G. Wodehouse. I have likewise omitted figures less intimately concerned with Camberwell than Alleyn, Lettsom and Ruskin whose lives have been dealt with at length by their own biographers. These include Charles Dickens' mistress, Ellen Ternan, whom he secreted at 16 Linden Grove, Nunhead, which, in his day, "still preserved an air of remoteness from metropolitan concerns", and Dr. Harold Moody who in 1931 founded the League of Coloured Peoples at 164 Queen's Road, Peckham.

I am very much aware of my debt, not only to the pioneering historical researches of D.H. Allport (1841) and W.H. Blanch (1875) but, even more heavily, to the no less learned and rather more systematic efforts of contemporary experts such as John D. Beasley, Mary Boast, Tim Charlesworth, Brian Green, Stephen Humphreys and Ron Woollacott.

What I have attempted to do is to complement their works and the various publications of Southwark Libraries, by relating together the development of areas which are elsewhere treated separately and wherever possible setting their story in the context of the development of London as a whole. If there is a dominant motif running throughout the text, therefore, it is the reciprocal relationship between the four areas considered and the great metropolis lying just to their north. Virtually every aspect of their past and present condition is an expression – economic, demographic or environmental – of that dynamic. This is most evident in the complex of processes conveniently lumped together by historians as 'suburbanisation'.

Indeed, H.J. Dyos' masterly study of the growth of Victorian Camberwell epitomised it as *the* archetypal suburb. In this, novelist George Gissing anticipated him by more than half a century, setting *In the Year of Jubilee* in De Crespigny Park, home of the fictional Peachey family and the ideal background for a tale of bourgeois pretension and skulduggery.

In writing this book, I have been aware of just how many fine buildings have survived the predations of neglect, developers, the war and enthusiastic local councils. Partly this is due to the fact that for a long time the area was not a popular choice for those who had money for development; and by the time it became more fashionable conservation regulations were in place. But in addition, Dulwich, Peckham and Camberwell have been well served by their active amenity societies. The role of the Camberwell Society, for example, is noted on p80 in the saving and restoration of Denmark Hill Station. Planning laws are all very well, but societies like these are vital in local affairs.

1. 'View of Camberwell from The Grove', published in 1776. In the distance the dome of St Paul's Cathedral is depicted, beyond the tower and cupola of St Giles', Camberwell's parish church. Grove House (now 45 Grove Lane) was once noted for its tea-garden.

The Rural Background

MEDIEVAL MANORS

As W.W. Hutchings remarked with majestic understatement in 1909 "on the whole the stream of national history left Camberwell severely alone."

Until Tudor times the parish of St Giles, Camberwell was occupied by a peasantry whose lives are only occasionally illuminated by surviving fragments of documentation. The first recorded mention of Dulwich – then Dilewysshe, 'the meadow where the dill grows' – dates from AD967, in a charter of the Saxon king Edgar. Camberwell is first recorded in the great Domesday Book survey of 1086. The lord of the manor was Haimo, Sheriff of Surrey. There was a church already in existence, though probably only built of wood, and, apart from sufficient land to employ eleven ploughs – perhaps 900 acres – there were also 63 acres of meadow and woodland sufficient to support sixty pigs, which largely fed themselves on acorns and beech-nuts. Peckham, unlike Dulwich, was also significant enough to be recorded separately in Domesday but had as yet no church of its own.

In 1127 Henry I granted the manor of Dulwich to the priory of Bermondsey, which lay a few miles to the north, athwart what is now the approach road to Tower Bridge, and was a foundation much favoured by royalty. The same monarch also granted lands in the Camberwell area to the splendidly named Sir Rothomago and Sir Reginald Poyntz. Shortly before their departure on the Second Crusade (1147-1148), these knights made their holdings over to Holywell priory in Shoreditch. As they held the rank of 'Freiherrn' of the Holy Roman Empire it has been suggested that this may account for the name of that manor becoming Friern Camberwell. More prosaically, the new association with a priory may itself be the source of the etymology, given that in Middle English *frere* could be used to describe a conventual occupant of either sex.

The parish church of St Giles, Camberwell is known to have been rebuilt in stone in 1152 by William, Earl of Gloucester, whose father, Robert, had married Mabel, granddaughter of Haimo. In 1154 the church was presented by William to "God and the monks of St Saviour, Bermondsey", which retained the right to appoint the vicar until its dissolution in the reign of Henry VIII.

Wrongdoing and routine administration supply further glimpses into the life of the medieval community. In 1235 outlawry was proclaimed on two

2. Domesday Book entries for Camberwell and Peckham.

3. A boundary marker which recalls the existence of the old Friern Camberwell manor. This marker, dated 1791, is now incorporated into the wall in Peckham Road, opposite the Town Hall.

local men for stealing bees and honey. Two women brewsters are known to have been in business locally in 1275 and the barley from which they made their ale was certainly one of the crops grown locally. In 1279 Gilbert de Clare, Earl of Gloucester, claimed, as manorial lord, the right to hold the Assize of Bread and Ale – i.e. fix the prices of those two basic commodities. The first vicar's name to be recorded dates from 1290. During that century the area is known to have been divided up into eleven estates.

Returns in the Lay Tax Subsidy rolls for 1332 -1334 show separate entries for Camberwell and Peckham and imply that both settlements were relatively prosperous. In the latter year what is now Croxted Road was recorded as Crokestrete (i.e. crooked or winding street), an important local thoroughfare which was probably a section of a pilgrim route ending at the great shrine of Thomas Becket at Canterbury. The Old Kent Road, running along the eastern edge of the modern borough of Camberwell, was an even busier road for pilgrims, noted for a watering-place named in honour of the saint and now commemorated by a Victorian public-house offering more ardent refreshment. This was also the site of an important gallows.

The earliest surviving records from the Dulwich manorial court, dating from 1333, suggest a village population of about a hundred. An early migrant from the City appears to have been Thomas Dolseli, a butcher and pepperer, who was clearly a person of major civic consequence, serving as an alderman, sheriff and, in 1357, Member of Parliament. The presence of four tile-makers in Dulwich between 1400 and 1420 implies either a quickening economic pace or improved standards of building as peasant incomes benefited from the scarcity of labour following repeated visitations of plague from 1349 onwards.

By the sixteenth century records of litigation over the clearance of woodland suggest that local landowners were wanting to respond to expanding metropolitan demand for food and other agricultural products. Woodland was a valued resource in its own right, providing the main constructional material for buildings, fences, tools and furniture, as well as fuel for hearth, oven and kiln. As such, it was systematically managed, with demarcated coppices of ten to twenty acres being cleared on a regular rotational basis every dozen years or so, then left to recover.

During the sixteenth century the number of distinguished residents multiplied as the expansion of London increased the number of office-holders and merchants seeking a semi-rural residence where they could relax, entertain and avoid periodic outbreaks of plague. Immunity from pestilence was not, how-

4. Old St Giles' parish church, destroyed by fire in 1841, the year in which this engraving was published.

ever, guaranteed. A major outbreak of plague in 1603, which carried off thirty thousand in the metropolis, accounted for 113 in the parish of Camberwell.

John Bowyer, a London lawyer, took up residence as lord of the manor of Camberwell Friern, which came to him as part of the dowry of Elizabeth Draper. Their brass memorial survives in St Giles' church, complete with a depiction of their eight sons and three daughters. The eldest son became a baronet and over the centuries the family accumulated lands stretching from Kennington to the Old Kent Road. Bowyer House survived on Camberwell Green until its demolition to make way for the railway in 1861. Another great local family was the Scotts. John Scott, one of the Barons of the King's Exchequer under Henry VIII, received the manor of Camberwell Buckingham after its owner, the Duke of that name, was executed in 1521. His brass is also to be seen in St Giles.

Tradition holds that Camberwell was a favoured hunting ground of King John and four centuries later of Charles I and his son Charles II. George, Prince of Denmark (1653-1708), consort of Queen Anne, is

5. Funeral brass of the prolific John Bowyer and his wife.

6. Bowyer House on Camberwell Green.

said to have had a hunting lodge at Denmark Hill. Certainly the treasurer of his household, the Earl of Wilmington, lived in some state at Camberwell Green. The hunting connection was maintained into modern times with the accommodation at Dog Kennel Hill of the Surrey Foxhounds.

SOUND INSTRUCTION

Another indicator of the emergence of a class of local residents well above the level of labourers and husbandmen is the establishment of Camberwell's first school, founded in 1615 by Edward Wilson, vicar of St Giles from 1578 to 1618. Explicitly established for the instruction of local boys – no parishioner's son to be refused entry – the school was also to offer free instruction to a dozen children of poor parents of the parish. Wilson's Grammar School originally stood on land donated by Sir Edmond Bowyer, east of St Giles' church, in which pupils were expected to occupy reserved seats in the north gallery every Sunday. Their master was required to possess the degree of Master of Arts and to be "sound in religion, body and mind, gentle, not hasty or furious, nor of evil example, sober, honest, virtuous and discreet, and of a wise, sociable and loving disposition."

Just over a century later the Greencoat School was "Erected to the Glory of God and the honour of the Church of England by Henry Cornelisen Esquire, in 1721" on Camberwell Green. Unlike Wilson's, which, as its name stated, was a grammar school, teaching Latin and Greek to aspirants to the learned professions, this was an establishment with humbler aims. Alarmed by the growth in the numbers of Quakers, Baptists and Congregationalists among the lower classes, the Church of England encouraged the creation of charity schools – Blewcoat, Greycoat, Greencoat – where the sons and daughters of the respectable working poor could receive a very basic education, indoctrination in the precepts of the Anglican faith and, implicit in the whole exercise, a clear understanding of their ordained place in society and the virtues required to accompany it – piety, honesty, diligence and obedience. The stone figures of model pupils which usually adorned such schools depicted them in the uniforms which were supplied free and prominently carrying a Bible and a testimonial to their unblemished character. (A charity school figure of 1785 can be seen at Archbishop Michael Ramsey School in Farmers Road). What was to become James Allen's Girls' School was likewise established in 1741 with a similarly humble purpose in mind: "to teach poor boys to read and poor girls to read and sew". It remained, in effect, merely a village school until 1858.

7. An elaborate Elizabethan monument to the Scott family in old St Giles's church.

8. Wilson's Free Grammar School at Camberwell.

9. The Greencoat School in 1800. Note the figures of 'charity children' placed above the doorways.

VERSAILLES AT PECKHAM

Sir Thomas Bond, favourite of Charles II and speculative builder of Bond Street (1684) in London's West
End, also built himself a handsome mansion at
Peckham, surrounding it with an imposing garden
in the formal French style. Bond would certainly
have seen such gardens while sharing the king's
exile and, in any case, he was married to a French
aristocrat.   He was also Comptroller of the Household (and, many hinted, *much* more besides) of the
Queen Mother, Henrietta Maria, who was also French.
The geometric and symmetrical French type of layout
was popularised around the metropolis by the nurs-
erymen and garden-designers, George London and
William Talman. Talman is known to have produced
architectural drawings for the Bond family and may
well have been personally responsible for the layout
at Peckham. Bounded by Peckham High Street, Hill
Street and Commercial Way, it boasted a parterre,
gravelled walks and lawns with a carefully posi-
tioned 'wilderness', modelled on the Elysian Fields
of the Tuileries in Paris. Not only were selected fruit
trees imported from France to adorn the garden,
there was even a French gardener to tend them. The

king himself, an enthusiast for French taste, was a
frequent visitor to Bond at Peckham. The diarist John
Evelyn (1620-1706), a connoisseur of gardens and
author of *Sylva* (1664), a pioneering treatise on
arboriculture, recorded in his diary (12 June 1676)
his admiration for Bond's "fine garden and prospect
through the meadows to London". A decade after
Evelyn's visit Bond's loyalty to the Catholic James
II was to cost him dear when his house was sacked
by a mob and, following that monarch's flight into
exile, forfeited to the Crown. Rocque's 1745 map of
London shows the garden retaining its original formal layout but both the mansion and its estate were
finally swept away in 1797 to make way for housing.

One of Bond's successors as a court favourite and
intriguer, Henry St John, Viscount Bolingbroke
(1678-1751), in 1725 built Friern Manor Farm
House, following his return from enforced exile in
France. Excluded from public life, he sought
consolation in letters and was a patron of Al-
exander Pope (1688-1744), who may well have
composed all or part of his celebrated *Essay on Man*
while staying at Friern Manor.

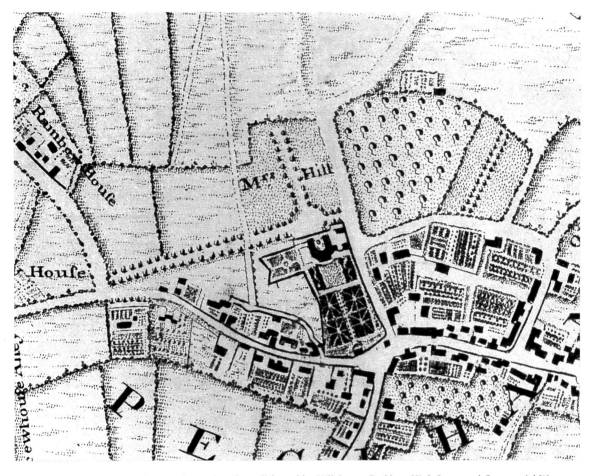

10. *Rocque's map of 1744-5, showing the Bond garden still framed by Hill Street, Peckham High Street and Commercial Way.*

ENTER THE EXOTICS

"Being sent at two years old to be brought up with my relatives at Peckham in Surrey, from them I received the first liking to gardens and plants. Their garden was remarkable for fine cut greens, the fashion of these times, and for curious flowers. I often went with them to visit the few nursery gardens round London, to buy fruit and flowers, and clipt yews in the shape of birds, men and ships."

The youthful migration of Quaker Peter Collinson (1694-1768) to his grandmother's home in Meeting House Lane in 1695 set the course of his adult life. Between 1650 and 1750 more than a thousand new plant species were introduced to Europe from other continents. Collinson was responsible for spreading more of them throughout England than any other man of his time, distributing seeds to correspondents in the provinces and encouraging young landowners to take an interest in gardening as "the most lasting of any occupation". Surely, he argued, it was "a pleasing scene for a man of fortune to behold the rising groves, barrenness made fertile, our country improved, ourselves made useful and happy, and posterity enriched." The Swedish traveller Peter Kalm made an expedition to Peckham in 1748: "a pretty village ... where Mr Peter Collinson has a beautiful garden full of all kinds of the rarest plants, especially American ones, which can endure the English climate and stand out the whole winter." Collinson was a close friend of Benjamin Franklin (1706-1790), who freely admitted that it was the Peckham plantsman who first awakened the interest in the phenomenon of electricity which later brought him a Fellowship of the Royal Society and acclamation as the inventor of the lightning-conductor. Collinson maintained strong links with many other acquaintances in the American colonies, advising settlers to cultivate hemp, flax, silk and vines and keeping them abreast of current scientific research in Europe. He was well placed to do so, being a

11. Henry St John, Viscount Bolingbroke; from the painting by Hyacinthe Rigand.

12. Peter Collinson - botanist, plantsman and antiquary.

member of the Royal Society, a founder member of the Society of Antiquaries and also much involved in both Kew Gardens and the infant British Museum. Although Collinson's famous garden disappeared long ago, he has a living memorial in Dulwich, where many of the horse-chestnuts, cedars and hornbeams planted by schoolmaster James Allen in 1741 were supplied from Collinson's Peckham plantation.

MARKET GARDENING

By 1600 Dutch and Flemish horticulturalists, refugees from Catholic persecution, were already settled along the Surrey bank of the Thames, from Battersea to Bermondsey, producing vegetables for the inhabitants of Westminster and the City on the other side of the river. These newcomers introduced new and better strains of standard English crops, such as cabbages, carrots, peas, beans and onions, as well as new plants, such as cauliflowers and pumpkins. More important still, they pioneered the use of 'hotbeds'—deep-dug trenches filled with dung and kitchen waste – to force early vegetables and salad crops. The chaplain to the Venetian ambassador noted in 1618 that enterprising immigrants had learned to turn a double profit by digging out underlying gravel, which they sold off as ships' ballast or as a building material, and replacing it with the "filth of the city ... as rich and black as thick ink." Sceptical natives initially feared that working land so intensively would ruin it. But progressive horticulturalists showed that

a man cultivating just three acres could not only support a family but employ extra labour as well.

By the 1660s London was surrounded by some 10,000 acres of market gardens. Within the parish of Camberwell, Peckham – enjoying the best access to the metropolis, via the Old Kent Road – was especially prominent in the business. The name of Melon Road commemorates one of the most highly prized of all commercial crops, a local speciality. Philip Miller. who worked at Kew and compiled the first great horticulturalist's handbook, *The Gardener's Dictionary* (1722), observed of melons that "there is not any plant cultivated in the Kitchen-garden, which the Gardeners near London have a greater ambition to produce early and in plenty." In 1717 a patch of ground was given to enlarge Camberwell's parish churchyard; its name – the Vineyard – may imply that grapes were once grown on the slopes of what is now Camberwell Grove. Marshy ground near Coldharbour Lane, on the west side of the parish, proved highly favourable to the growing of osiers (willows), as the name of Tenpenny's Great Osier Farm bore witness. The osiers created a valuable side-employment, being woven into baskets for transporting local produce up to the markets of the metropolis. By 1745 local barley was used for making beer at a brewery which stood on the site now

13. *A farm at Camberwell Green c.1815.*

14. *Old Camberwell Mill, one of two in the parish, an essential facility for an agricultural community.*

15. *Regency elegance – well-dressed residents depicted by local artist J.B. Cuming, c.1820. The house, built c.1709, may occupy the site of the former manor house of the Manor of Milkwell; it was demolished in 1851-2 to allow an approach road to be built to a new Congregational Church. Wren Road, named for the architect of St Paul's, now covers the site. His association with Camberwell was traditional but undocumented.*

16. *The Thomas à Becket public house on the Old Kent Road commemorates a watering-place for the horses of pilgrims en route to Canterbury. Nearby stood a celebrated gallows.*

occupied by the filling-station on Peckham Road, between the Town Hall and Camberwell College of Art.

The predominantly rural nature of mid-eighteenth century Camberwell can be seen quite clearly from the local Friern Manor map of 1739 and from the relevant section of Rocque's overall survey of the capital, made in 1745.

Market gardening was so important that in the eighteenth century Camberwell vestry paid bounties for the destruction of pests which damaged crops – sixpence a bushel for caterpillars, threepence a dozen for sparrows, fourpence each for hedgehogs and a shilling for a polecat. In 1809 Manning and Bray, authors of a *History of Surrey*, observed of Camberwell that "in the pasture a great number of cows are kept which not only supply the inhabitants of this place with milk but furnish a good deal for London." In 1811 the Revd. Daniel Lysons reaffirmed the local importance of horticulture and its reciprocal relationship with the market and waste of the metropolis: "the soil in general is fertile, and is much improved with manure, which is procured easily, and in great abundance from London." And as late as 1853 the *Illustrated London News* could still run a special feature on Friern Manor Dairy Farm, a major enterprise whose 186 cows grazed over two hundred acres and provided employment for thirteen male milkers, who worked in a state-of-the-art gas-lit parlour.

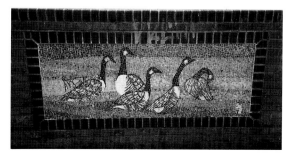

17. *Goose Green – a mosaic in a children's playground commemorates the rural past of East Dulwich.*

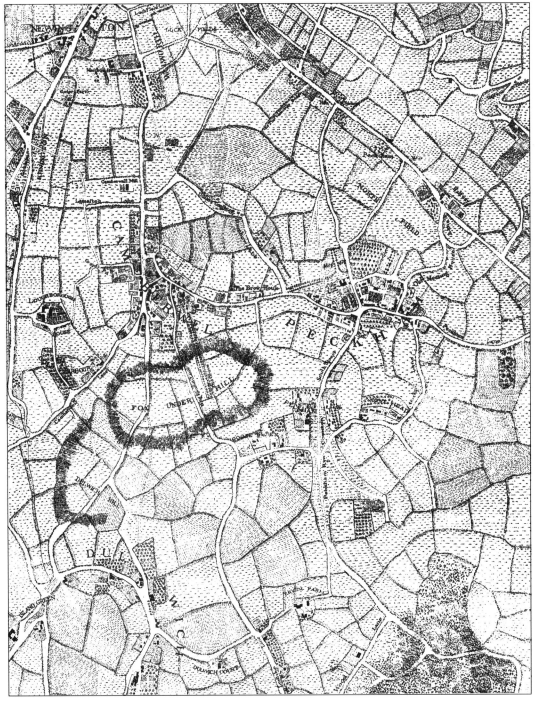

18. *Camberwell parish still very much a rural community. A section of John Rocque's map of the environs of London, 1744-45 showing a patchwork of fields with the smaller, more intensively cultivated clustered around Peckham and along the line of the Old Kent Road at the top of the map. Road junctions provide local points of settlement at both Camberwell and Peckham which are almost joined by 'ribbon development' along the road betwen them.*

Edward Alleyn: from Actor to Benefactor

Edward Alleyn, like his contemporary William Shakespeare, was a man who, despite a relatively modest social background and without benefit of a university degree, used his theatrical and entrepreneurial talents to make himself both rich and respected. Born on 1 September 1566 in the parish of St Botolph, Bishopsgate, on the north-eastern edge of the City of London proper, Alleyn was the son of an innkeeper who later became the head of the City's mental hospital, Bedlam. The family traumas of Alleyn's childhood, although by no means exceptional, may well have contributed to his personal piety by reminding him that the possibility of sudden death was ever present. By the time he was a teenager he had lost his father, a step-father, three brothers and a step-brother.

Although Alleyn's second step-father, John Browne, was a well-established haberdasher, Alleyn apparently declined to join the family business and at seventeen was off touring the provinces as an actor with the Earl of Worcester's Men. In 1586 he is known to have appeared in a moralising pantomime on the theme of *The Seven Deadly Sins*. By 1589 he is recorded as being in partnership with a surviving brother, John, and the actor Robert Browne (apparently not a relation), and to have been jointly purchasing with them 'playing apparel, playbooks, instruments and other commodities'. By 1592 Alleyn was a leading light with the Lord Admiral's Men, whose patron was Charles Howard, Earl of Nottingham. In that same year he married 21-year-old Joan Woodwarde, step-daughter of Philip Henslowe who was henceforth to be his business partner. Henslowe, illiterate but shrewd, was a man of diverse interests, a dyer and a pawnbroker and, much more to the point from Alleyn's perspective, owner of the Rose theatre. As the plague raged through the capital, closing the playhouses, for much of the first year of their marriage Alleyn was on tour in the provinces. Six surviving letters to his illiterate wife, who replied through Henslowe's hand, reveal much affection and an equal amount of anxiety, lest she, too, fall victim to the pestilence then ravaging the Bankside theatre district where they had their home.

By 1594 Alleyn was the acknowledged star of the Lord Admiral's Men, specialising in larger-than-life roles which enabled him to exploit his above-average

19. Edward Alleyn (1566-1626).

height and booming voice. Renowned for his performances in the name parts of Christopher Marlowe's *Tamburlaine the Great* and *Dr. Faustus*, he also excelled as Barabas in the same author's *The Jew of Malta* and as Orlando in Robert Greene's *Orlando Furioso*. No less a critic than acid-tongued Ben Jonson wrote a fulsome paean to Alleyn's skill in thundering verses, praising him as the only actor to surpass the ancients:

> And present worth in all dost so contract
> As others speak, but only thou dost act.
> Wear this renown, 'Tis just, that who did give
> So many poets life, by one should live.

MASTER OF THE BEARS

During the 1590s, Alleyn prospered sufficiently to make major investments in commercial properties and the highly profitable business of bear-baiting, which took place between theatrical entertainments along Bankside. By 1597 Alleyn's property portfolio was so extensive that for several years he gave up the stage to manage his investments full time. Resuming his dramatic career in 1600, he made his

20. Dulwich College in 1776 - the earliest known view.

last documented public appearance in 1603, appropriately representing 'The Genius of the City of London' during the celebrations which accompanied the coronation of James VI of Scotland as James I of England. By then Alleyn had too many business commitments to allow him to pursue a stage career as well. In 1600, in partnership with his father-in-law Henslowe, he had built a new theatre, the Fortune, on the north side of the City, in the parish of St Giles without Cripplegate. He also took on leasehold properties in Kennington and at Firle in Sussex.

In 1604 Alleyn finally obtained a long-coveted official appointment of the Mastership of the Bears, which gave him the authority to schedule and supervise baiting at the Bear Garden on Bankside and at the royal palaces of Greenwich and Whitehall, as well as occasional lion-baiting in the royal menagerie at the Tower of London. The breeding of the mastiffs used in baiting was another lucrative sideline, as they were highly prized by private owners.

LORD OF DULWICH

In 1605 Alleyn was able to buy the lordship of the Manor of Dulwich from the impoverished Sir Francis Calton, whose family had bought it for £609 in 1544, after Henry VIII had confiscated it from the Abbey of Bermondsey. The purchase price was now a princely £5,000. Calton subsequently appears to have felt that he had let the side down, socially

speaking, by selling to a self-made man and to have communicated as much to Alleyn. Alleyn brushed his reproaches aside with a breezy self-confidence:

"And where you tell me of my poor original and of my quality as a player. What is that? If I am richer than my ancestors I hope I may be able to do more good with my riches than ever your ancestors did with their riches ... That I was a player I cannot deny; and I am sure I will not. My means of living were honest, and with the poor abilities wherewith God blessed me I was able to do something for myself, my relatives and my friends. Many of them now living at this day will not refuse to own what they owe to me. Therefore I am not ashamed."

As if to compound his claim to social eminence Alleyn also purchased the neighbouring Rycotes estate, creating a domain of some 1,100 acres, stretching from Denmark Hill to Sydenham Hill and from Lordship Lane to Croxted Road.

Despite his purchase of Dulwich, Alleyn for several years continued to reside in the parish of St Saviour's, Southwark, where he had become a person of great consequence, serving successively as tithe-collector, auditor, churchwarden and magistrate. Around 1612, however, Alleyn at last removed from his home in the shadow of the Bishop of Winchester's Thames-side palace and took up residence at the manor house, Hall Place, in Dulwich.

FOUNDING OF THE COLLEGE

Alleyn was now determined to devote his time to his pet project, a charitable institution which would combine a school for a dozen poor children with almshouses for a dozen poor pensioners. Inspiration for this may well have come from the 'Hospitals' for orphans and the elderly founded in Amsterdam in 1611, as copies of their statutes were found among his papers. Another example from the same year, but much closer to home, was Sir Thomas Sutton's Charter-house, established in a refurbished former monastery on the northern edge of the City of London. Alleyn was therefore putting himself in the company of the elite, as Sutton was reputed to be the richest commoner in the realm.

The building contract for the College of God's Gift was signed in May 1613 and the chapel was consecrated three years later, on Alleyn's fiftieth birthday, by no less a personage than the Archbishop of Canterbury himself. Building was completed the following year and staff recruited – a Master and Warden and four Fellows to serve respectively as preacher, schoolmaster, usher and organist. Alleyn's statutes required that the dozen poor scholars, six poor 'sisters' and six poor 'brothers' should be nominated by the clergy of the four parishes with which he was most closely associated – St Botolph's, Bishopsgate, where he had been born and brought up; St Giles, Cripplegate, where his greatest single investment, the Fortune theatre, stood; St Saviour's, Southwark, long the site of his marital home; and St Giles, Camberwell, within whose boundaries he now resided. A formal patent of incorporation, constituting the College as a legal entity and enshrining its regulations, was not achieved until 1619, when Alleyn himself stood in the College chapel to boom out the details of the Deed of Foundation and Statutes in the presence of assembled dignitaries. These included the Lord Chancellor, Francis Bacon, and the distinguished architect Inigo Jones, whom Alleyn probably knew from his work as a designer of sets and costumes for extravagant court masques. The proceedings were rounded off by a banquet at which the guests consumed more than a hundred different dishes, ranging from eels, oysters and ducks to capons, rabbits and artichoke pie.

TROUBLES IN OLD AGE

The closing decade of Alleyn's life was clouded by vexations. In 1616 William Henslowe, brother of his late father-in-law and business partner, and John Henslowe, Philip's nephew, contested Philip Henslowe's will, alleging that, as he lay dying, Alleyn had bamboozled his father-in-law into signing a new document, depriving John of his just share of his uncle's legacy. In addition to this Alleyn poured £1,500 into a fruitless venture to build a playhouse, Porter's Hall, in the stylish residential district of Blackfriars. The stylish residents opposed the enterprise and Alleyn found himself additionally embroiled in a dispute with the lessor of the property, who eventually returned his £1,500 at the behest of the Court of Exchequer in 1623. In the meanwhile another disaster had occurred with the burning down on the Fortune at midnight on the 9 December 1621. Although it was swiftly rebuilt Alleyn reduced his involvement to that of a one-twelfth shareholder.

Joan Alleyn died on 28 June 1623 and was buried in the College chapel. Before the year was out Alleyn had remarried. His bride, Constance Donne, was the daughter of the celebrated poet and preacher John Donne, Dean of St Paul's Cathedral, who lived much of the time at the Peckham manor house of his brother-in-law, Sir Thomas Grymes. As Constance was almost forty years younger than Alleyn the match struck contemporaries as decidedly odd. Alleyn, however, seems to have been less than besotted, as the negotiations over her marriage portion of £1,500 were coldly business-like and his legacy to her, apart from that lump sum, was limited to her personal jewellery and £100.

Alleyn died on 25 November 1626, a few months after attaining his sixtieth year, and was buried two days later in the College chapel.

Alleyn's memory, and his theatrical and family connections live on in the names of roads in the Dulwich area which commemorate Henslowe, his partner, the tragedian (Richard) Burbage, Shakespeare's business partner, the dramatist (Thomas) Dekker and (Joan) Woodwarde, his first wife. Townley Road is named for Alleyn's thrice-married mother, born Margaret Townley. Tylney Avenue is for Edmund Tylney, Master of the Revels to Elizabeth I, to whom Alleyn had to apply for licences to act in certain plays in 1583, when his career was just beginning. Adys Road recalls John Adey or Adys, a resident of Goose Green, who served Alleyn as a legal adviser. Aysgarth Road refers to a parish in Upper Wensleydale where Alleyn bought an estate, Simondstone, in the summer of 1626. The strain of the journey he undertook to inspect Simondstone in July of that year may well have precipitated his final illness.

21. *The First Surrey Rifle Volunteers, Brunswick Road headquarters. These were opened by the Earl of Lovelace, Lord Lieutenant of Surrey, in July 1865. The 150-foot drill hall was complemented by a four-acre parade ground.*

A Changing Parish

DEFENCE OF THE REALM

Although special responsibilities for defence devolved on coastal areas, every parish was expected to make its contribution to the nation's war capacity. In 1533 Camberwell was ordered to establish butts for archery practice. A muster return of 1558 showed that Camberwell could raise five archers and the same number of billmen, Peckham five archers and one billman and Dulwich four billmen only. Forty years later the respective contributions had greatly expanded. Camberwell now had eight pikemen, ten billmen and five bowmen, Peckham thirteen pikemen, nine billmen and four bowmen, and Dulwich eight pikemen, ten billmen and nine bowmen. This reflected, no doubt, the expansion of population which characterised the late sixteenth century. It may also represent a tightening-up in the enforcement of military obligations. If so, standards fell so badly in the following decades that in 1629 fines were imposed because there were no bows and arrows locally available for practice.

A century and a half later, at the height of the wars against revolutionary France, Britain daily anticipated invasion. Camberwell, like hundreds of other communities, in 1798 raised its own garishly-uniformed volunteer militia, officered by leading local residents. The commander was Claude Champion de Crespigny, the medical officer the distinguished physician John Coakley Lettsom. The contingent stood down following the truce established by the Treaty of Amiens in 1802.

A renewed fear of French hostilities prompted the formation of volunteer rifle regiments in the 1850s. From 1865 onwards Camberwell's force – the First Surrey Rifle Volunteers – was headquartered in a handsome, purpose-built drill hall in Brunswick Road. Not until the second Boer War of 1899-1902, however, would its members see active service.

ALWAYS WITH YOU: POVERTY AND ITS RELIEF

From Tudor times onwards the relief of poverty was primarily the responsibility of the parish, supplemented by the voluntary efforts of individuals and corporate bodies. The Camberwell churchwardens' accounts for the period 1670-1720 reveal those causes of poverty deemed worthy of succour at public expense. Domestic catastrophe prompted a donation of sixpence "To a poor woman that was burnt out." By contrast, the insanity of Elizabeth Long and her protracted confinement in Bethlem hospital in

22. Old Camberwell Workhouse. This stood in Peckham Road and was superseded c.1816 by a larger building in Havil Street. Fit inmates were required to contribute to their upkeep by performing simple industrial tasks and growing vegetables in the garden.

London led to substantial and recurring expenditures as high as £1. 13s. 0d. Perhaps concern to prevent another such burden prompted the three shillings and sixpence granted to "Hugh Moulsey that was out of work and like to fall into despair." Loss of status, rather than employment, prompted the gift of a shilling "to a decayed gentleman". Widow Grove was granted thirty shillings in recompense for the unforeseen expenses she had incurred as a result of "the wench that dyed there" and five shillings was allocated for nursing a baby found abandoned under a haystack.

Patriotic gestures were regulated by a keen awareness of social rank. A shilling was judged appropriate for "a disabled officer out of Flanders" but half that was enough for a licensed mendicant, "a poor soulger and his wife with the Lord Mayor's pass." Finally, payments were sometimes prompted by the desire to draw a final line under a source of continuing expense, as in the case of sixpence "given to a

sick man to avoyde further charge."

An entirely extraordinary charge upon the parish occurred in 1710 when thousands of German Protestant refugees, hounded from the Rhineland Palatinate by Louis XIV of France, fled to England and were temporarily housed in tented camps at Blackheath and in Camberwell. A special relief fund was raised and a Mr Cock was appointed as a trustee to distribute it. Churchwardens also hired barns to shelter, presumably, infants and the infirm. Many of the newcomers were encouraged to move on and make a new life in Ireland, the West Indies or North America.

In 1727 the Camberwell Vestry "finding the number of their poor daily increasing" built a workhouse in Peckham Road to accommodate them. In 1815 it was replaced by a much larger building in Havil Street. The daily diet specified for inhabitants in 1838 was twelve ounces of bread and a pint of milk, supplemented with a weekly allowance of one and a half

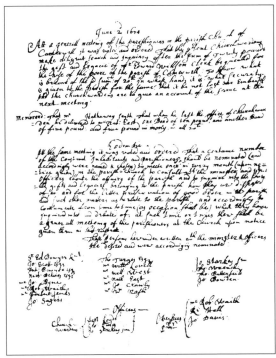

23. *The minutes of a Camberwell Vestry meeting in 1674. The main concerns were the relief of the parish poor and the "better preservation of good order". The signatures of those attending are headed by Sir Edward Bowyer and John Scott Esq.*

BUILDING MATERIALS,
CAMBERWELL.

A

CATALOGUE

OF ALL

The valuable Building

MATERIALS

Of the old Workhouse,

BELONGING TO THE PARISH OF ST. GILES,

CAMBERWELL, SURREY,

And a nearly-new additional

BUILDING

Adjoining the same, with Sheds, Workshops, &c.

To be taken down at the Purchasers Expence.

WHICH WILL BE

Sold by Auction,

BY

Mr. Samuel Closs,

ON THE PREMISES,

On TUESDAY, 18th of MARCH, 1817,

AT ELEVEN O'CLOCK.

24. *Sale of the old Workhouse materials, 1817.*

pounds of meat and the same of potatoes, rather less of suet pudding and a few ounces of tea and sugar, plus four pints each of soup and gruel.

CRIME AND VICE

Pre-modern policing was a hit and miss business. Householders were required to serve as nightwatchmen on a rota basis or send one of their servants as a substitute. Returns surviving from April 1639 show that on Monday, 1 April all four Camberwell householders liable for service that night sent servants in their place while the three, presumably poorer, Peckham men on duty were obliged to go in person. Paid parish constables administered the rota and also took responsibility for moving vagrants on until they were returned to their original parish of settlement, which was deemed to be liable for their relief. Constables also enforced royal decrees against unlicensed alehouses and – an offence particularly prevalent in the environs of the burgeoning metropolis – against householders who "Devide theire howses and receave in undersitters and Inmates, a great meanes of increasing the poore."

'Undersitters' were liable to be migrants from the countryside, seeking work in or near the metropolis. There was also an intermittent reverse flow of metropolitans seeking 'recreation' in hopefully discreet locations beyond the prying eyes of their neighbours. Elizabeth Cresswell (1625-1685), who was brought up in Camberwell and maintained a long-term relationship with Sir Thomas Player, a Member of Parliament, provided a range of 'services', including flagellation, for his circle of acquaintance at a Camberwell establishment punningly known as 'Oates' Boarding School'. A contemporary squib boasted brazenly of the alleged scale of its operations:

There shall all Provision be made to entertain the
  best.
Old Mother Cresswell of our Trade
For to rub down our Guest
Three hundred of the briskest Dames in Park or
  Fields e'er fell
Whose am'rous Eyes shall charm the Flames
Of the Saints at Camberwell.

Minor offenders could be confined to the Dulwich Village 'cage', which bore the inscription "It is sport for a fool to do wickedness; thine own folly shall correct thee." There was another cage in what was the yard of the Joiner's Arms, now 33 Denmark Hill. Next door stood a watchhouse for the village watchmen. Public humiliation meant exposure in the stocks, outside the workhouse in Peckham Road. The correction of vice usefully supplemented the parish income. The same churchwardens' accounts for 1670-1720 record fines being levied for 'disorders', drunkenness, 'prophane cursing and swearing', 'tipling in servise time' and even for disturbing divine worship by thrashing a child in the churchyard. The same accounts show spasmodic major disbursements for the legal expenses involved in pursuing serious wrongdoers:

– in 1699 for presenting baker William Bensted at the Kingston Quarter Sessions for "makeing the Poor's bred to light" (he was fined but seems to have kept the parish contract to make bread for the poor);

– in 1713 for "taking a woman supposed to have murdered her bastard child and fled";

– in 1716 for "the examination, commitment and prosecution at Ryegate Assizes of Joseph Weston who was hang'd for Robing the Church".

Even more shocking – or fascinating – to contemporaries was the case of Camberwell man George Barnwell who, incited by Sarah Millwood, "a wanton of Shoreditch", murdered his uncle. This incident inspired a play by George Lillo (1693-1739) entitled *The London Merchant, or, The History of George Barnwell*. Dickens was fascinated by this 'affecting tragedy', regularly recited it as a boy and refers to it in *Great Expectations* and other novels.

ARMS AND THE MEN

Seen in the larger context of the London region as a whole, the pattern of law-breaking was by no means as random as such fragmentary evidences might suggest. There was a clear correlation between harvest failures, high bread prices and the level of thefts and robberies driven by destitution and desperation. The ending of major wars released thousands of ex-servicemen onto the labour market, especially in London and the south-east where many garrisons and bases served as points of discharge. The ending of the War of the Spanish Succession in 1713 may therefore indirectly help to explain why in 1715 the leading residents of Camberwell had become so anxious about their security that they agreed to pay a supplementary subscription to reward any persons successfully apprehending criminals who should subsequently be convicted.

Another surge of crime might have been expected after the ending of the American War of Independ-

ence in 1783. In 1788 a regular patrol was instituted to watch the streets. In 1789 Camberwell parish church was robbed. This incident prompted leading residents to issue a comprehensive tariff of rewards to encourage the apprehension of malefactors who even *intended* to rob the church or "broke into *or out of* any dwelling-house, shop, warehouse, granary, barn, stable, coach-house, cow-house, dairy, fowl-house or outbuilding."

The following four decades, a period of revolutionary politics and warfare on a continental scale, witnessed a vicious cycle of felony and retribution through which the fear and anger of the propertied vented itself by visiting savage punishment on those luckless enough to be caught for anything more than the most trivial offence. The Vagrancy Act of 1797 was used to harass the long-established gypsy community which inhabited the woods at Norwood. On one occasion the Chief Constable disguised two of his men as aristocrats and another two as their liveried footmen, then had them drive up to the gypsy encampment, where they were soon surrounded by the locals, who expected rich pickings but instead found themselves with a fight on their hands. On another occasion twenty officers made a dawn raid and "threw down the tents of the encamped gypsies and carried off the occupants in several hackney carriages waiting in readiness."

In 1800 two highway robberies took place on Dulwich Common within the space of a single hour. In 1802 eccentric Samuel Matthews, a reclusive jobbing gardener known 'the Dulwich Hermit', was brutally murdered for no apparent reason. In 1804 one George Heeles was found guilty of robbing the house of Mr Epps of Camberwell and sent to the gallows for making off with a tea-pot. In 1807 the Vestry offered an extraordinary reward of forty guineas "for the conviction of the person who committed an outrage upon a poor girl in the northfields." In 1811 a watchmaker was stopped by three muggers and relieved of his coat, watch and money. When he and a second man urged the local watchman to abandon his wooden shelter on Champion Hill and join them in giving chase, the guardian of the law declined the invitation and the ne'er do wells made good their escape.

In 1812 a horse patrol, armed with pistols and cutlasses, was instituted, primarily to escort travellers along the lanes between Dulwich and the dropping-off points of coaches plying to and from London. An Enclosure Act in that same year deprived the Norwood gypsies of access to much common land which had been essential to their subsistence livelihood. It was reported in *The Times* the following year that "representations having been made of various depredations committed in the neighbourhood of Dulwich and Sydenham by large parties of

313

$\mathcal{A}$ Table of Fees or Dutyes to be
From time to time paid to the Minister
Churchwardens Parish Clerk Sexton
& Made and agreed upon by the
Parishoners of the Parish Of
Camberwell in the County of
Surry at a Vestry called For that
Purpose held on the 26th Day of
December in the Year of our
Lord 1735

£ s d

The Ministers Dues

	£	s	d
For the Burial of a Corps in the Church or Vault under the Church, Church Porch or Vestry		5	-
For the Burial of a Corps in the Church yard with attendance at the house		5	-
Without attendance at the house		3	-
For every Marriage		5	-
For Churching a Woman			-
Going to Baptize a Child at home		2	6

The Parish Dues

	£	s	d
For the Burial of a Corps in the Vault under the Church above the age of Six year	1	5	-
For the Burial of a Corps in the Vault under the Church under the age of Six years		15	-
For opening the Vault and making it good again		10	-
For Tolling the Bell		1	-
For the Burial of a Corps in the Church yard above the age of Six years		1	-
For the Burial of a Corps in the Church yard under the age of Six years		1	6
For the little Bell			6
For the Pall if used		5	-
For the Burial of a Corps in the Church Porch or Vestry Room	2	10	-
For the Burial of a Corps in any part of the Church except the Vault		10	-

W Griggs. Photo Lith.

25. *A table of fees payable to the vicar, churchwardens, clerk and sexton, in the parish of Camberwell in 1735.*

gypsies who have assembled there for some time past, a party of officers were despatched to scour the country and took eight into custody including their queen."

When a quarter century of war with France ended in 1815 and 400,000 men were demobilized and thrown onto the labour market a further upsurge in crime was anticipated. In Camberwell an emergency force of special constables was recruited and yet another prosecution reward fund raised. In September 1816 an extraordinary meeting of the Vestry resolved that "endeavours should be made to procure this parish to be included within the limits of the Bow Street patrol." And the prosecutions went on. In February 1818 one Dawkins appeared at the Old Bailey, charged with stealing a shirt and three handkerchiefs from Mr Acland's laundry. For this he was sentenced to transportation to Australia for seven years.

PITY THE POOR

Philanthropy also had its role to play in underpinning public order and in 1803, following the failure of the Peace of Amiens and the renewal of war with France, leading local residents such as Mr De Crespigny, Dr Lettsom and Dr Wanostrocht launched a subscription fund in aid of a "Society for encour-

aging and aiding the industrious sick and aged poor of the village of Camberwell." During its first year of operation the Society set fifty-six women and children to demonstrate their industriousness by knitting worsted into stockings or spinning flax into thread. Twenty-two expectant mothers were loaned boxes of household linen, which were "returned in good time and in good order." They were also among the recipients of "825 quarts of broth, sago, caudle and other nutritious things" distributed to some "three hundred persons in poverty and distress." In 1804 Mr De Crespigny hosted at Champion Lodge what was then called a 'fête-champêtre', but might now be called a 'fund-raiser', to raise money for the needy. Five hundred attended and the guest of honour was no less an eminence than the Prince of Wales who "after inspecting the articles for sale on the many booths ... and going on a brief tour of the grounds, withdrew, whilst the remainder of the guests returned to the lawn for dancing."

A MEET PLACE FOR MEETINGS?

The Parish Vestry was originally so called because it met in the vestry of the parish church. But it also met in more convivial surroundings - such as The Golden Lyon, The Green Man, The Artichoak, The Grey Hound, The Father Redcap and the Kentish

26. The old Vestry Hall, opened in 1827.

27. *The new Camberwell Vestry Hall, opened in 1874.*

Drovers. Writing in 1875 local historian W.H. Blanch, who was also Assistant Overseer of the Parish Vestry, observed sternly" it might perhaps be thought extraordinary were our justices of the peace to hobnob nowadays with the chairman of the vestry at a public house, but such a thing has taken place in this parish." The absence of formal Minutes relating to such meetings no doubt awakened the darkest bureaucratic suspicions in this upright functionary. But his own researches would have confirmed that his was a decidedly novel way of looking at public business. Supporters of the Green Coat School had regularly held their annual audit at The Butchers' Arms, while the Peckham trustees for lighting gathered at The Red Bull. As late as 1838 even such ultra-respectable persons as a group of Quakers thought nothing inappropriate about "meeting at the Bull Inn, Peckham, for the purpose of forming a Literary and Scientific Institute in that village."

Blanch's criticism had already been met, however, long before he wrote his book. A vestry hall was opened in 1827 which, according to him "was very hot in summer and particularly draughty in winter. Externally an abortion, it was internally an infliction on all concerned..."

MORE RESPONSIBILITIES, MORE POWERS

The year before Blanch published his magisterial history of *Ye Parish of Camerwell* his employers had taken possession of a newly-built Vestry Hall which embodied a growing civic pride and had been necessitated by their increasing responsibilities. London's population doubled between 1841 and 1881 and Camberwell's population grew even faster, prompting an extension of local government functions. Camberwell's first District Surveyor was appointed in 1845. A decade later Parliament passed the Metropolis Management Act which conferred on Camberwell Vestry enlarged powers over sewerage, drainage, paving, cleansing and lighting. Within two years the reformed vestry had opened a municipal cemetery and had saved Camberwell Green from being built over. In 1864 London's main drainage system finally reached Camberwell. The year afterwards Camberwell vestry assumed responsibility for the neighbourhood's former turnpike roads.

28. 'A View of London from Camberwell', 1797. At first glance this seems much like the similarly sylvan view of 1776 (see Ill. 1). But an intermittent line of tall houses can be seen stretching across the picture in the middle distance. Significantly, the one at the far left is shown to be still in the course of construction, surrounded by scaffolding. Between it and the houses to its north stretch meadows with conical piles of cut hay.

New Links to London

BRIDGES AND ROADS

For the first seventeen centuries of the capital's existence London Bridge was the only bridge across the Thames. Southwark and the Borough, at the southern end of the bridge, therefore became the nucleus from which the metropolis would spread southward to engulf previously distinct village communities like Camberwell, Peckham and Dulwich. This process was decisively accelerated by the construction of two new bridges, at Westminster and Blackfriars, in 1750 and 1769 respectively. These not only eased the previously congested flow of traffic from one side of the river to the other but also encouraged the development of industry on what had for centuries been the open fields of Lambeth Marsh. Roads to the south began to show dramatic evidence of ribbon development, as Walter Harrison noted in his 1776 *New and Universal History ...of London and Westminster*: "the spirit of building ... appears to have equally affected this part with any round the metropolis; for between Newington Butts and Camberwell several new streets have been formed and a prodigious number of buildings erected."

Partly in response to this thickening out of the residential population, in 1782 the well-made turnpike road leading out of the capital was extended from Newington to Camberwell Green; from there two further branches reached out into Peckham and the northern fringes of Dulwich. The parish authorities in Camberwell responded to the increased flow of traffic by upgrading its simple transport infrastructure. New milestones were put in place in 1772; and in 1776 and 1787 Acts of Parliament were secured to authorize new arrangements and expenditure for street-lighting and 'watching' (i.e. policing) in Camberwell and Peckham respectively. In 1797 the nuisance to traffic of pigs being allowed to "range at large in the roads" prompted the offer of a five shillings reward for identifying their owners.

In 1789 John Morgan of Penge erected a tollgate to charge travellers passing along the road he had had built through the fields he leased from Dulwich College. His lease ended in 1809 but the College decided to maintain the operation for its own profit – and still does, to the annoyance and amusement of motorists. In the same year new finger-posts were erected around Dulwich for the guidance of travellers. In 1811 the Reverend Daniel Lysons observed in his account of Camberwell that "... the village has been uniformly increasing and at no period so rap-

29. Milestone on Red Post Hill.

30. The Dulwich tollgate at the beginning of this century.

idly as within the last ten years. It has the reputation of being healthy and is a very commodious situation for those persons who, from inclination, or for the benefit of the air, are induced to prefer a country residence, though business calls them daily to the metropolis."

Within a few years of these words being written the pace and scale of house-building expanded and quickened with the opening of three new bridges over the Thames at Vauxhall (1816), Waterloo (1817) and Southwark (1819), and the consequent construction of the Camberwell New Road (1818), soon to be lined with terraces of sober brick family residences.

By 1800 regular daily coach services were already running from Camberwell into the city centre and commuting had therefore become a feasible proposition, at least for the local elite. The traffic between Camberwell and the metropolis was, however, by no means restricted to the workaday journeys of well-to-do residents. Readers of Jane Austen will readily recall how even an expedition of a few miles to view a 'prospect' would become for her characters the occasion of elaborate preparations, extensive discussion and eager anticipation. In the pre-railway age a journey by horse or carriage, especially involving mixed company, the elderly, the young or the feeble, was necessarily a time-consuming exercise.

31. *Camberwell Fair 1801. The company is shown respectably dressed and decorously behaved.*

Only fit men might reasonably be expected to ride at 'post haste' speed. Eight miles an hour was reckoned a good rate for a professionally driven stage-coach on the open road, with regular relays of fresh horses. A private party might expect to make perhaps half that, especially where they were relying on the same team to take them to their destination and back the same day.

Allowing time for negotiating one's way through the tangle of London's streets, Camberwell and Dulwich lay at just about the right distance for a day out in the country for city-dwellers. A number of the parish's larger hostelries therefore provided extensive facilities for day-trippers from the capital. A ballad of the reign of George II specifically mentions The Green Man at Dulwich in the same verse as the famous pleasure-gardens at Vauxhall and Ranelagh. In 1748 this "noted house of good entertainment" had a bowling green and "a handsome room for breakfasts, dancing and entertainment." The Rosemary

Branch at Peckham had grounds extensive enough for patrons to amuse themselves with cricket, horse-racing or pigeon-shooting. The Greyhound had eleven acres – enough for gardens, two cricket fields and stabling for twenty-six horses. The White Hart, completely rebuilt in the 1770s, had a clubroom with a Portland stone chimney-piece and an ornamental plaster ceiling. Denmark Hall, erected at the top of Denmark Hill by Southwark wood-carver Luke Lightfoot, was named in compliment to Christian VII of Denmark, who visited England in 1768. Large parties initially came down from London to view its most noted feature – one of the largest rooms in the country, thirty feet wide and a hundred feet long. But the novelty soon wore off as did the takings and so it was converted into houses and later demolished.

Peckham High Street had a flourishing theatre in the 1790s, offering the standard popular fare of farce and melodrama. In 1799 a play in three acts was published under the title *The Peckham Frolic or Nell*

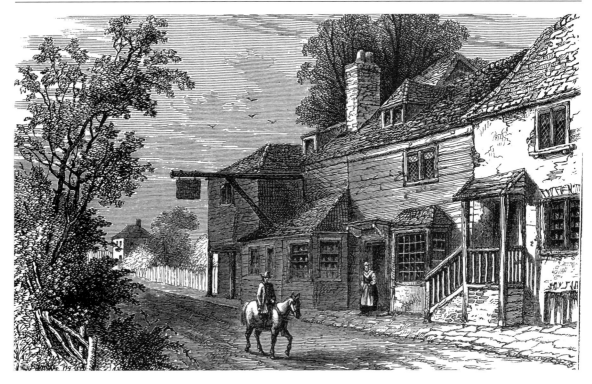

32. The Old Rosemary Branch.

33. The Old Greyhound, Dulwich, at the beginning of this century.

34. The Plough Inn, in Lordship Lane.

Gwyn. The actor and minor dramatist John Baldwin Buckstone (1802-79) made his youthful debut there in *The Dog of Montargis* before eventually going on to become manager of the Haymarket theatre in the capital. By 1819, however, the Peckham venue was being referred to as "half theatre, half barn" and by 1822 "the old theatre" had evidently closed and the building occupied by Peckham Lancasterian School for Boys.

Grove House (later Camberwell Hall) was celebrated for its tea-gardens, which attracted the more respectable elements of society. In 1801 it was described as "well adapted as a place of public entertainment, and much frequented by genteel companies." Some excursionists, however, contented themselves with mere sottishness and gluttony. By 1787 Camberwell parish, though still largely rural in aspect, already had thirty-three public houses; and for years The Plough in Lordship Lane proudly displayed an inscription in one of its windows: "March 1810. Thomas Mount Jones dined here; ate six pounds of bacon, drank nineteen pots of beer."

GENTLEMEN AND THEIR RESIDENCES

According to the neighbourhood's most distinguished resident, the eminent physician J.C. Lettsom, "in Camberwell village there are few poor inhabitants ... They consist chiefly of respectable merchants and tradesmen, and those holding eligible offices in the public service." One such 'officer' was John Relfe, musician to George III, who lived in Church Row, Camberwell. Another was Sir John Knight, an admiral, no less, whose estate sprawled over the whole of what became Bushey Hill Road and would eventually be covered by more than two hundred houses. Such men could often afford not only to build, but to build well. If ribbon development of brick terraces and rows of villas characterised the building boom on the immediate fringe of London, further south, and most notably in Dulwich, imposing new residences were being built on an altogether grander scale for altogether grander occupants. Bell House (1767) was built for Alderman Thomas Wright, Master of the Stationers' Company and Lord Mayor of London in 1785. Belair was built in 1785 for John Willes; a century later Blanch boldly attributed the design to "Mr. Adams" (i.e. Robert Adam), although Pevsner, while conceding its 'handsome proportions', asserts no such claim.

35. Belair, built in 1785, and traditionally attributed to Robert Adam.

36. This monument to Lord Mayor Brass Crosby, some time resident of Dulwich, once stood in St George's Circus on the approach road to Westminster Bridge. It has now been relocated outside the Imperial War Museum, Lambeth.

Another Lord Mayor, Brass Crosby, lived more modestly, with 'only' two acres of grounds – until he married a great fortune and promptly removed himself from Dulwich. Crosby had won national renown in 1770 by defying Parliament when it had sent an officer to the City to arrest a printer who had dared to publish an account of its proceedings. As Chief Magistrate of the City, Lord Mayor Crosby declined to execute the warrant and, for upholding the liberty of the press, got himself confined to the Tower of London. His release was greeted with a torchlight procession of triumph and he went on to confirm his popularity by defending inhabitants of the City from the depredations of the Royal Navy's press gangs. His grateful fellow citizens honoured him with a handsome obelisk which once stood prominently in the middle of St George's Circus, on the approach road to Westminster Bridge, but has since been sidelined to the park abutting the Imperial War Museum.

Three of the finest houses in the parish were built by successful lawyers. Casino (*a.k.a.* Casina) House, Denmark Hill, built for Richard Shaw, the solicitor who organised the defence of Warren Hastings during his celebrated seven year trial. The house allegedly cost £40,000 – pretty much the fee he had been paid for his professional services in that titanic encounter. The design of the house has been attrib-

uted to John Nash and the garden, with greater
certainty, to Humphry Repton. Later inhabitants
included Joseph Bonaparte and Lord Mounteagle.
Casino Road commemorates its departed grandeur.

Kingswood House was built in 1812 by William
Vizard, legal adviser to the colourful Queen Caroline
of Brunswick during her tumultuous divorce proceedings with King George IV.

The third property was erected for the famously
irascible Edward Thurlow (1731-1806). Despite being
sent down from Cambridge for obstreperousness,
and conducting a thirty-four year affair with the
daughter of a coffee-house keeper, he rose to become
successively Solicitor General, Attorney General and
Lord Chancellor, as well as a trusted confidante of
the Prince of Wales. Following his loss of office,
Thurlow devoted himself to serious spending, buy-
ing over a thousand acres of land to create an estate
which stretched from Herne Hill almost to Streatham,
and commissioning the fashionable architect Henry
Holland to build a mansion on a site now bounded
by Thurlow Park Road and Elmcourt Road. While
construction went on Thurlow installed himself at or
near the former Green Man tavern. His mistress lived
in Dulwich and unblushingly attended divine service
in the College Chapel, like any respectable local
matron.

Holland took three years to complete his Knight's

38. *Lord Thurlow.*

37. *The house built by Lord Thurlow at Knight's Hill. It took three years to build and went seriously over budget. Thurlow
refused to live there and the house was soon demolished.*

39. *Casino House – a villa in the grand style. The picture dates from c.1870, a century after it was built.*

Hill assignment, which went three times over budget. The enraged Thurlow vowed never to enter his dream house and when presented with his architect's bill forced Holland to accept arbitration at the hands of City Surveyor George Dance and royal architect James Wyatt, who decreed a reduction in Holland's fee "the work not being well done". The house was eventually demolished and its materials sold for a quarter of the cost of construction.

A particularly fine range of Georgian mansions still stands along the eastern edge of Dulwich Village. No. 97 was built in 1796 by John Adcock, No. 101 in 1760 by Noble Spring, No. 103 (Marlowe House) in 1759 by Mrs. Lydia Normandy and No.105 (Woodlawn) in the same year by Moses Waite. Pond House, also built in 1759 for John Tinkler, although now much altered, extended and converted into flats, still retains its imposing central pediment and elegant Venetian window. Glenlea (1803-4) manages to combine a battlemented parapet with an Ionic pedimented portico and half-bow-windows, the whole unified by a liberal application of stucco. Its designer, George Tappen, surveyor to Dulwich College, exhibited the design at the Royal Academy and also built The Willows and Northcroft in 1810.

40. A handsome pair of semi-detached villas of c.1790 on Camberwell Road. It was a common fate for such houses to have their front gardens built over to create commercial premises.

41. 'Heaton's Folly' on the road from Peckham to Nunhead. Lysons relates that the owner, Mr Heaton, employed out of work local men to build a mound and the house on top as a philanthropic gesture in hard times.

Socially, the increase in the number of gentry resident in Dulwich was marked by the establishment in 1772 of the Dulwich Society, an exclusive dining club, initially limited to twenty four members. Economically, the presence of significant purchasing power encouraged the establishment or enlargement of businesses providing goods and services for the 'carriage folk'. The smithy which stood at what is now the corner of Calton Avenue was rebuilt in 1760 and extended in 1792; another was built in 1765, near where No. 76 Dulwich Village now stands. A shoemaker's opened in the same row in 1783 and a painter and glazier's in 1800. In 1780 a coach-building and wheelwright's business was started, appropriately on the site later occupied by Park Motors in Boxall Road. In 1791 the village butcher extended his grazing land from eight to twenty-eight acres. A decade later the wheelwright decided to rival him by diversifying into butchery on the side.

ARCADIAN ACADEMIES
Apart from its regular schools, Georgian Camberwell was also home to a number of small, private academies, usually maintained by maiden or widowed ladies or by clergymen, according to the gender of their pupils. These provided tuition and accommodation to the offspring of the gentry in sylvan surroundings, well removed from the dangers to health and morals represented by the metropolis.

The novelist and dramatist Oliver Goldsmith (1728-74) endured three years as an usher in Peckham under Dr Milner, a Presbyterian minister, who obliged him to share a bed with the French teacher. Goldsmith later looked back on the humiliations of this period with undisguised bitterness: "The usher is generally the laughing-stock of the school. Every trick is played on him; the oddity of his manners, his dress or his language, is a fund of eternal ridicule; the master himself now and then cannot avoid joining in the laugh; and the poor wretch ... lives in a state of war with all the family."

As a child the poet Byron spent two years under the tuition of Dr. Glennie, who was much impressed with his charge's intellectual precocity: "his reading in history and poetry were far beyond the usual standard of his age." Unfortunately Glennie's instruction in Latin according to the then prevailing Scottish system had to be entirely undone when Byron moved on to Harrow, though the damage was doubtless mitigated by the fact that Byron appears to have been a persistent truant, evading the classroom to play at brigand in Dulwich Woods, in imitation of local gypsies.

Peckham Collegiate School, established around 1770 by Baptist minister Dr Martin Ready in the chapel adjoining his house in Peckham High Street, trained the distinguished non-conformist preachers Richard Slate and Dr Thomas Raffles, who had long and successful careers in Preston and Liverpool respectively. Under Dr Thomas Ready it received as a weekly boarder, from the age of seven to fourteen, the future poet Robert Browning (1812-1889).

No illustrious pupil is associated with the name of the Belgian Dr Nicholas Wanostrocht (1745-1812), a successful author of school textbooks; but he was sufficiently eminent for his passing to be marked by the erection in Camberwell parish church of a fine funerary monument by John Flaxman, the foremost monumental mason of his era. The academy Wanostrocht had established in 1795 was carried on by his son and his illustrious cricketing grandson (see p.115) until its removal around 1830 to Blackheath.

A boarding school for young ladies run by a Mrs Ellis was known to have flourished in the 1780s. Dr Lettsom's handsome residence became, after his death, a similar establishment, known as Pelican House. At

43. Goldsmith House, where the young Oliver Goldsmith worked as an usher.

Myrtle House, 13 Queen's Road, Peckham, the Misses Clifton ran a ladies school in the former home of royal physician Sir Benjamin Brodie. Such institutions continued to be regarded as adequate for young children and teenage girls until well into the nineteenth century. The future statesman Joseph Chamberlain attended Miss Pace's school in Camberwell Grove in the 1840s, along with the

42. Dr Glennie's Academy in 1820.

44. Denmark Hill Grammar School.

future African explorer (Sir) Harry Johnston.   In 1850 Mrs Tattershall's Manor House Ladies' School was still in existence.

In *Dombey and Son* (1848), Walter Gay attends a weekly boarding school at Peckham (chap. IV). In the same novel Mr Feeder boards there "with two old maiden ladies" (chap. XIV).

As the century progressed and nepotism gave way to more meritocratic methods of recruitment in business and public life, older boys were expected to meet more exacting standards in schools organised and staffed on more professional lines. Such institutions included Denmark Hill Grammar School which, from 1837 to 1873, occupied a seventeenth-century house on Denmark Hill, and Camberwell Collegiate School for Boys which, from 1834 to 1867, was housed in purpose-built premises modelled in the style of an Oxbridge college. An altogether more specialised education could be obtained in the 1860s at Allison Towers, Dulwich Common, where a dozen or so young gentlemen with military ambitions prepared themselves for glory under the supervision of Herr Woolenhaufst.

AN INDUSTRIAL NUCLEUS

It was the construction of yet another link with London – the imposingly named Grand Surrey Canal – that initiated Camberwell's exposure to the industrial age. The first section was opened in 1811 and a branch, stretching out at right angles towards Peckham, was completed in 1826. Its most important freight was timber, the demand for which soared with the mid-century building boom which created modern Camberwell in the railway era. Alongside the canal other industries connected with building, such as brick kilns, soon developed. The lime works of E.R. Burtt & Sons, established in 1816 to convert limestone into quicklime for cement, continued in

45. The South Metropolitan Gas Works, Old Kent Road, c.1904.

46. *The Surrey Canal near the Old Kent Road, c.1930.*

business until the 1960s. For the delectation of bourgeois palates there was an ice-house where ice, imported from Scandinavia in winter, could be preserved for sale the following summer. Other canalside factories later developed to manufacture linoleum, paints and glue. Cheek by jowl with these rather noxious establishments were other works making comestibles such as jam, roasted peanuts and mineral water. The canal was finally closed and filled in in 1970.

The other major industrial intrusion was the South Metropolitan Gas Company. Founded in 1829, it established a major gasworks on a 36-acre site in the Old Kent Road and began operations in 1833. Its first business was to provide gas-lighting for streets and business premises, but from 1842 onwards the villas of the local wealthy could also enjoy the benefits of modern illumination. Gas not only gave a much better light than candles but was also more economical. Just one penny bought fifty-two hours of brightness, whereas, with candles costing sixpence a pound, a pennyworth of candlelight only lasted for just under

six hours. Although it was therefore much cheaper to light a house with gas than with candles, the initial cost of installation was enough to keep it out of the homes of the local poor for another half century, most acquiring the facility between 1892 and 1905. The South Metropolitan Gas Company would by then be providing work for some six thousand employees, who, thanks to its presiding genius, Sir George Livesey (1834-1908) would also be benefiting from one of the earliest profit-sharing schemes. Livesey's other benefactions included the first free library in the locality.

Thanks to the canal and the gasworks, therefore, the streets of North Camberwell thus acquired a distinctly lower working-class character, housing those who wished to live within a short walk of work, or could not afford to live elsewhere. In 1889 social investigator Charles Booth was to describe Sultan Street, between Bethwin Road and Wyndham Road, as "one of the vilest slums in the whole of London".

A Quaker Hippocrates

Camberwell's single most distinguished resident in the last quarter of the eighteenth century was the physician John Coakley Lettsom (1744-1815). He has been cruelly memorialised in a rhyme as unjust as it is flippant:

> When any sick to me apply
> I physics, bleeds and sweats 'em
> If after that they choose to die
> Why verily   ... I Lettsom.

The pun may have been irresistible but the judgment was a slur on the name of a man who was an adornment to his profession and a benefactor to thousands.

Lettsom was born, the son of a Quaker plantation owner, on the remote island of Little Jost Van Dykes, Tortola in the West Indies, now part of the Virgin Islands.   As a Quaker Lettsom was barred at that time from politics and the law and therefore from advancement via the intrigues of either the Court or the courts. Quakers progressed in eighteenth century society through business or learning, but without benefit of attendance at either Oxford or Cambridge, from which their religion likewise excluded them.

Shipped off to a Quaker school in England at the age of six, Lettsom at sixteen was apprenticed to Abraham Sutcliffe, a Quaker practising as both a surgeon and an apothecary in Settle, Yorkshire. Sutcliffe instructed his apprentice not only in medicine and the Latin which was still its essential accompaniment, but also in botany and geology, thereby nurturing in him the interest in natural phenomena which was to make him such a zealous horticulturalist and collector of scientific specimens.

Having completed five years instruction, Lettsom came to London in 1766, bearing a letter of introduction from his master to the eminent Dr John Fothergill, who took him on as a 'surgeon's pupil' at St Thomas's Hospital, then located in the Borough, just south of London Bridge. After a year, however, Lettsom was obliged to break off his training and return to the West Indies to sort out the family estate following the death of his father.

Lettsom's legacy from his father consisted of slaves, but he had learned from Dr Fothergill that slavery was an abomination and therefore he set them all free, thereby depriving himself of his entire inher-

47. *Dr John Coakley Lettsom, engraved from a drawing from life.*

itance. Unperturbed, Lettsom used his medical training to found his future fortune. Accepting that other planters still regarded *their* slaves as property rather than people, Lettsom played on the fact that they represented *valuable* property and conducted for his neighbours what might nowadays be called a crash screening programme, which netted him no less than £2,000 in just six months. Half he gave to his mother, retaining the rest to return to Europe and continue his studies.

Encouraged no doubt by his Caribbean success, Lettsom now aspired to rise higher than an apothecary or surgical assistant and set himself to acquire university qualifications, studying first at Edinburgh and then at Leyden in the Netherlands, neither of which institution discriminated against Quakers. During this period of clinical education Lettsom distinguished himself by making careful case-notes on each individual patient he saw, an apparently unprecedented procedure which his teachers and fellow-trainees regarded as decidedly eccentric. Graduating M.D. in 1769, Lettsom became a Licentiate of the Royal College of Physicians in 1770, being thereby qualified to practise in the City of London and within seven miles radius of it. Marriage that same year brought the young physician a wealthy wife and useful connections in the mutually supportive Quaker community.

48. *Dr Lettsom's house at Grove Hill.*

Lettsom inaugurated his career by opening a General Dispensary in Aldersgate Street at the western edge of the City of London. It was a ground-breaking innovation. In the absence of hospital out-patient departments, which scarcely then existed, Lettsom's dispensary offered the urban poor a clinical facility which for the first time enabled them to be seen by a practitioner of consultant rank. Even more revolutionary was the willingness of the consultant to visit, in their own home, those too sick to move. Further even than this, Lettsom volunteered to provide free medical treatment for the poor wretches imprisoned for debt near his dispensary in the Wood Street Compter.

Lettsom's pioneering example soon proved its worth and he himself calculated that by 1800 more than forty such dispensaries were functioning in other parts of the metropolis and major provincial cities. But Lettsom also realised that the routine of the dispensary provided a daily parade of just those ailments which a doctor would most often have to deal with and therefore constituted an ideal training-ground for the medical student. He was sufficiently enthused by this 'internship' concept to draft a complete syllabus based on the idea but nothing came of it until the year of his death, when the

Apothecaries Act prescribed fifteen months attendance at a dispensary as a minimum "evidence that the candidate for licence has passed through a sufficient course of practical medicine."

In 1773, still only twenty-nine, Lettsom took the lead in founding the Medical Society of London to bring together thirty each of the capital's leading physicians, surgeons and apothecaries. Unlike other contemporary associations, which were largely personal cliques, the Society was sufficiently broadly based to avoid petty factionalism and to survive the death of its founder.

Lettsom was also a member of the first committee of the Royal Humane Society, which was founded in 1774 to promote life-saving from drowning through the use of artificial respiration. He remained associated with the Society for the rest of his life, fund-raising, propagandising, supervising its finances, drafting its annual reports and organising its annual dinner – which included a procession round the table of those "who had been raised from the dead" thanks to the Society's efforts each year. Lettsom's other charitable interests included the Philanthropic Society for the Prevention of Crimes, the Society for the Discharge and Relief of Poor Persons Imprisoned for Small Debts, the Institution for the Relief and Em-

49. Dr Lettsom with his family. Note the greenhouse and potted plants, suggestive of his botanical interests, and the classical urn, symbolic of his taste and learning.

ployment of the Indigent Blind and the Asylum for the Indigent Deaf and Dumb.

Energetic and enterprising, Lettsom earned well, building a large personal practice. Taking no holiday for nineteen years and continuing to dress in the simple style of a Quaker, he doubtless felt justified in making his domestic circumstances as agreeable as possible. In 1779, after systematically surveying the environs of the capital, Lettsom settled on Camberwell to build himself a country residence – a fine three-storied villa, Grove Hill. Its fourteen rooms included a superb study suite consisting of an interconnecting hothouse, library and museum. This accommodated the doctor's 6,000 books and vast collections of coins, shells, minerals, bones and natural history specimens. From the roof there was a breathtaking 360 degree view, to the north as far as Harrow-on-the-Hill, to Shooter's Hill in the east, beyond Chelsea to the west and as far as Sydenham Hills to the south – a panorama which, in Lettsom's

own words, combined "naval grandeur and rural elegance, nowhere equalled in the world, being indisputably the richest scenery that was ever afforded to the sight."

Visitors were greatly struck by the elegance of Grove Hill's grounds, which boasted a Temple of the Sybils and a statue of Venus, sculpted by the Veronese artist John Baptist Locatelli (1735-1805), then working locally in the Lambeth area. There was also a boating lake, skirted with weeping willows, with a fountain in the middle. Little wonder that Grove Hill inspired a long descriptive poem from the Revd Thomas Maurice ending:

> Such are the soft enchanting scenes displayed
> In all the blended charms of light and shade
> At Camberwell's fair grove and verdant brow,
> The loveliest Surrey's lofty hills can show.

50. Another view of Lettsom's Camberwell Grove Hill villa in 1805. Notice especially the classical motifs cast in artificial Coade stone. Mrs Coade, owner of the family business, which was located on Lambeth Marsh, died in Camberwell.

But Lettsom's little kingdom also had a decidedly practical aspect, incorporating a kitchen garden, an orchard and two hothouses, producing apricots, peaches, figs, grapes and mulberries. Encouraged no doubt by his old mentor Fothergill, and perhaps by the earlier example of Collinson's 'plantation', Lettsom became an assiduous collector of plants from overseas. Those that could be cultivated in his garden were systematically labelled with their Latin and English names. The rest were incorporated into his *Hortus Siccus* ('dry garden') collection of dried plants, which filled an entire section of his library, assembled into sixty volumes. Lettsom, who had started out with two and a half acres, eventually extended his holdings to more than ten, establishing an experimental area where he pioneered the growing of Continental fodder-crops, such as mangel-wurzel and sea-kale, hoping to provide English dairy-farmers with a winter food for their herds. Although the site of Lettsom's villa and estate was subsequently covered by Nos. 9 to 12 Grove Park, as late as 1950 an acacia, cedar and catalpa from his day is said to have survived in their gardens.

Lettsom's last major institutional commitment was, like his dispensary, a single-handed personal initiative. Sea-bathing had become a much-favoured therapy, especially for skin diseases and tubercular infections, such as scrofula. But it was only available to those who lived at the coast or could afford to travel there. In 1791 Lettsom, therefore, founded the Royal Sea-Bathing Hospital at Margate to provide supervised medical treatment for the poor, utilising the therapeutic properties of sun and sea – in effect the first open-air sanatorium in the modern world.

Lettsom, although he lectured and published prolifically on a wide range of topics, from bee-keeping and prison reform to the medicinal uses of tea, has been belittled periodically by some medical historians because he made no major original contribution to medical knowledge except a description of the peripheral neuritis associated with chronic alcoholism. But Lettsom was a discerning judge of others' work and did not shrink from controversy. When the Royal Humane Society was split over the advisability of accompanying artificial respiration of the chest with inflation of the lower intestine with tobacco smoke (by inserting a bellows in the anus!) Lettsom consistently opposed this ancillary 'stimulation' and, after the death of its champion, Dr. Hawes, had the recommendation rescinded. When Jenner's discovery of vaccination was challenged by another claimant, Lettsom inaugurated the Royal Jennerian Society in his defence.

Lettsom's generosity, both as a host and and as a philanthropist, inspired some inspired doggerel from James Boswell, the biographer of Samuel Johnson:

51. Coade stone motifs from Lettsom's demolished villa. These now adorn business premises in Camberwell Road.

"Methinks you laugh to hear but half
The name of Dr. Lettsom;
From his of good – talk, liquors, food,
His guests will always get some.

And guests has he, in every degree
Of decent estimation;
His liberal mind, holds all mankind
As an exalted nation.

....

West Indian bred, warm heart, cold head,
The City's first physician;
By schemes humane, want, sickness, pain,
To aid is his ambition.

From terrace high, he feasts his eye,
When practice grants a furlough,
And while it roves o'er Dulwich grove
Looks down – even upon Thurlow. * "

In 1800 Lettsom's income was a fabulous £12,000 in a single year. But even this flow could not keep pace with his free-handed lifestyle and in 1810 he was obliged to sell Grove Hill. His last years were, however, to be unclouded by financial anxieties. True to form Lettsom was soon rescued by another tremendous stroke of good fortune, inheriting a legacy worth £10,000 a year in 1812. In that same year, already a Fellow of the Royal Society of forty years standing, he was elected President of the Philosophical Society of London. Nevertheless, despite his wealth and many institutional commitments, the restless Lettsom continued to work as a physician, dying in harness, as it were, from an infection contracted while conducting a post-mortem examination. The doctor's contemporary standing may be judged from the fact that a description of Camberwell in a guidebook of 1819, *The British Traveller*, records its only distinction as having within its boundaries the residence of the "late famous Dr. Lettsom."

* *Edward, Baron Thurlow (1731-1806), Lord Chancellor (1778-83), then living at or near the former Green Man tavern while a house was being built for him at Knight's Hill.*

52. *The interior of the Dulwich Art Gallery at the beginning of this century.*

Galleries and Artists

AN ENGLISH FIRST

Dulwich Picture Gallery is England's oldest public picture gallery. The nucleus of its collection was the legacy of Edward Alleyn to Dulwich College, consisting of family, royal and theatrical portraits. They included pictures of medieval and Tudor monarchs and of sibyls, allegorical figures representing prophecy and wisdom. In 1686 the College received another bequest of paintings, this time from William Cartwright, another actor, whose father was one of the lessees of Alleyn's Fortune theatre. Visiting the collection in 1791, Horace Walpole, connoisseur, aesthete and snob, dismissed it as consisting merely of "a hundred mouldy portraits".

The College holdings were greatly enlarged in 1811 when Sir Francis Bourgeois, a Royal Academician and Landscape Painter to George III, left 371 pictures to the College. Many of these had been collected from 1790 onwards by art dealer Noel Desenfans for a projected national gallery in Warsaw, a project brutally terminated by the extinction of the Kingdom of Poland itself in 1795. Desenfans, unpaid, hung on to the collection, displaying many of them at his Charlotte Street home until his death in 1807, when they passed to Bourgeois on condition that he find

an institution which would put them on public display. Bourgeois himself was to die soon afterwards, in December 1810, following a fall from his horse, but lingered long enough to make hasty arrangements with the College through the mediation of a personal friend, the distinguished actor John Philip Kemble, and a College Fellow, Robert Corry.

Although Bourgeois thoughtfully bequeathed £10,000 for the upkeep of the collection and a further £2,000 for work on the College's existing gallery, the College, with the support of Mme Desenfans, decided to finance the building of a new, purpose-built gallery. The architect engaged was Sir John Soane (1753-1827), then at the height of his powers and reputation. Soane, son of a Reading stonemason, had studied under the City of London's surveyor, George Dance, and had been awarded a scholarship by George III which enabled him to travel for three years in Greece and Italy, grounding himself thoroughly in Classical architecture. In 1788 he had won the competition to design a new Bank of England, the most prestigious project of his era, and in 1806 he was elected to a Professorship at the Royal Academy.

Soane's simple and severe design for the Dulwich project, constructed between 1811 and 1814, consisted of a sequence of five top-lit galleries, partly inspired by the type of picture-gallery then fashion-

53. *Noel Desenfans*

54. *Sir Francis Bourgeois.*

able in country houses. Three of the galleries are square, two oblong and, although they flow one into another, they are sufficiently divided to achieve what the doyen of Georgian architectural history, Sir John Summerson, has called "quasi-independence of its neighbour". For Summerson "the building as a whole reaches a level of emotional eloquence and technical performance rare in English, or indeed in European architecture."

One of the most unusual and striking features of the gallery is the mausoleum. This dominates the centre of the facade and houses the mortal remains of its benefactors M. and Mme Desenfans, Bourgeois and Soane himself. While this might strike the modern mind as slightly bizarre, the gesture merely followed a precedent established at the time, Desenfans having been originally interred in a similar mausoleum, designed by Soane, at the rear of his Charlotte Street residence. Soane had moreover a deep and learned interest in funerary monuments. The mausoleum he erected to his wife in 1815 in Old St Pancras churchyard is a smaller version of the Dulwich scheme, probably inspired by an ancient Alexandrian catacomb, whose details had been published in 1809. Completing the chain of influences, the depressed dome on the St Pancras version was allegedly an inspiration for one of the

crucial elements of Sir Giles Gilbert Scott's seminal 1924 design for the 'classic' red telephone kiosk.

The success of the Gallery has necessarily involved considerable modification of Soane's original creation. The almshouses, built either side to house elderly ladies, were converted to galleries and offices in the 1880s. In 1912-15 an additional range of galleries was added to the east of Soane's original building to accommodate further bequests and in 1937-8 yet another (now demoted to house the lavatories). Severely damaged by a flying-bomb in 1944, the Gallery was restored (1947-1953) by Sir Edward Maufe and Arthur Davis. The idiosyncratic architectural critic Ian Nairn was less than happy with the result: "the restoration, though exact, is oddly unsympathetic." But Nairn had only a qualified regard for the original, anyway: "One of Soane's most original, least satisfying designs ... an intellectual solution, a beautifully played game of chess ... a great curiosity, not a masterpiece." In 1980 the Gallery was redecorated in accordance with Soane's original colour scheme, burnt sienna and grey-green walls offsetting gilded edges to arched apertures. Soane's creation retains its iconic status among architects. A competition launched in 1990 for designs for additional facilities attracted no less than 377 entries.

55. Dulwich Art Gallery – the mausoleum. Note the funerary urns and sarcophagi.

The actual gallery collection was breezily described in 1966 by Ian Nairn as being "completely conventional but of high quality: the kind of selection that would appear in any big country house but without the same distressing proportion of duds." Cunningham's 1849 *Handbook of London* was more reverential, noting especially the twenty-one canvases by Teniers, nineteen by Cuyp and five by Murillo. Other artists represented less plentifully at that date included Rembrandt, Rubens, Van Dyck and Hobbema among the Dutch and Flemish masters, Titian, Veronese and Caravaggio among the Italian and Watteau, Claude and Poussin among the French. The *Handbook* warned intending visitors sternly: "Without a ticket no person can be admitted, and no tickets are given in Dulwich. Schools and children under the age of fourteen are not admitted." This did not, apparently, apply to Robert Browning, who claimed to have visited the gallery regularly as "a child, far under the age allowed by the regulations." The 'prior ticket only' system was abandoned in favour of general free admission from 1858 onwards.

THE WATER COLOURISTS

Water-colour painting reached a new height of popularity in England in the first half of the nineteenth century, establishing itself as a peculiarly English medium of artistic expression. In part this arose from professional artists' technical interest in the medium, which led to its recognition as a distinctive field of endeavour. In 1804 the Society of Painters in Water-Colours was founded and, soon after, a rival organisation, the Associated Artists in Water-Colour, was established. Its emergence provoked the original institution to re-style itself the *Old Water-Colour Society*.

Another factor contributing to the water-colour vogue was its widespread use to record botanical, zoological or archaeological specimens and architectural or landscape features – all subjects in which educated people were expected to take an interest. Drawing was one of the few disciplines widely studied by both sexes in polite society and also formed an essential part of the professional training of military and naval officers, physicians and surveyors. From drawing to water-colour was but a short step and teachers and publications soon proliferated to cater to growing public demand. It is therefore unsurprising that Camberwell, with its genteel resident population and plethora of minor academies, should prove an attractive area of residence for artists seeking customers or pupils.

David Cox (1783-1859) was born in Deritend, a manufacturing quarter of Birmingham but moved to London in 1804 and supported himself by scene painting for London theatres so that he could study under John Varley (1778-1842), one of the foundation members of the Old Water Colour Society, a member of William Blake's circle and author of *Landscape Design* (1816). Cox also had the good fortune to know the brilliant Thomas Girtin (1775-1802), whose technical innovations had already begun to revolutionise water-colour landscape painting before his tragically early death. Cox's own abilities were recognised by the influential publisher, Rudolph Ackermann, who was skilfully cashing in on the fashion for art as an amateur 'accomplishment'. Ackermann's *New Drawing Book of Light and Shadow, in Imitation of Indian Ink* (1809) contained no less than twenty-four illustrative aquatints by Cox.

Cox soon began to prosper as a teacher and went on to lay the foundations of both his fortune and his reputation by turning his lessons into manuals such as *A Series of Progressive Lessons in Water Colour*, which ran to nine editions between 1811 and 1845. By 1810 he had become president of the Associated Artists in Water-Colours but in 1812 joined its rival, the Old Society. From 1815 to 1827 Cox lived in Hereford, teaching drawing at a girls' school, but he returned to London to settle in Camberwell from 1829 to 1841. During this period he wrote several theoretical works, most notably a *Treatise on Landscape Painting and Effect in Water Colours* (1841).

Even more influential than Cox's writings, perhaps, was a minor but significant innovation from his Camberwell period. In 1836 Cox began to paint on a rough Scottish-made paper, intended to be used for wrapping parcels, but eminently suited to the broad surface effects characteristic of his painterly style. A similar paper was subsequently manufactured commercially for the art trade and marketed as 'Cox Paper', *The Oxford Companion to Art* summarises Cox's career with mild condescension: "His paintings of country scenes with their anecdotal homeliness were popular in the later nineteenth century. His style in water-colour was versatile with occasionally penetrating observation." Cox finally left Camberwell to retire to Harborne, near his native Birmingham, a convenient base for his annual sketching tours to the Welsh mountains. In his later years he concentrated increasingly on painting in oils.

Samuel Prout (1783-1852), born in Plymouth, came to London at twenty and soon found work making copies of works by Turner and Girtin. Befriending Cox, he also compiled educational works for Ackermann and moved south of the river, settling

56. Sir John Soane, painting by Sir Thomas Lawrence.

in Stockwell in 1811. Supporting himself by teaching, Prout finally found his métier in the 1820s, specialising in Continental street-scenes. Over the course of his career he exhibited more than five hundred water-colours. In 1845 Prout was sufficiently prosperous to move to 5 De Crespigny Terrace, where he lived until his death, much comforted by the friendship and warm regard of his near neighbour, John Ruskin, whose personal collection included nearly as many water-colours by Prout as by Turner.

Henry Gastineau (1791-1876), while still a young man, built himself a house, Norfolk Lodge, in Coldharbour Lane, and lived there for the rest of his long life. An enthusiastic teacher and prolific and workmanlike artist, Gastineau exhibited his work for no less that fifty-eight seasons, producing nineteen paintings in the last year of his life and dying the last survivor of the original members of the Old Society of Painters in Water Colours.

CAMILLE PISSARRO

Camille Pissarro (1830-1903), like Claude Monet, came to London in 1870 as a refugee from the Franco-Prussian war. His house at Louveciennes, west of Paris, was occupied by Prussian troops for four months. Billeting themselves in the bedrooms, they stabled their horses in the ground floor rooms and

57. David Cox, by an unknown artist.

used his canvases as door-mats. Of fifteen hundred paintings that he had been forced to abandon – representing twenty years work – only forty survived. In London he would manage to paint just a dozen pictures – and have two of them rejected by the Royal Academy.

Monet and Pissarro explored London's galleries together, keen to see the works of England's legendary landscapists, Constable and Turner, but actually finding themselves more impressed by the more recent output of the Pre-Raphaelite Dante Gabriel Rossetti and society portraitist G.F. Watts. When it came to painting, however, they pursued separate tracks. Monet set himself to depicting such well-known central London sights as the Houses of Parliament, the Thames Embankment and Green Park. Pissarro, by contrast, settling in Upper Norwood – "a charming suburb", he recollected thirty years later – painted much the same sort of prosaic scenes from his surroundings as he had been doing on the fringe of Paris – suburban streets, parks, even railways, focusing on "the effects of fog, snow and springtime". It was all rather un-British, the sort of subject-matter normally only tackled in London by hack artists working for illustrated magazines or manufacturers of cheap souvenir prints. Pissarro's environment was a microcosm of the suburbanisation which was

absorbing traditional settlements and eroding ancient countryside. One of his best known paintings – *Lordship Lane Station* – now in the Courtauld Institute, stresses the confrontation of old and new as a steam locomotive and track thrust outwards towards the onlooker from the centre of the picture and rows of raw suburban houses pause on the horizon, poised to envelop the open countryside which the railway has sliced through. *Fox Hill, Upper Norwood,* by contrast, still wears a distinctly rural aspect as a small party of strollers move away from the onlooker up a winding unpaved village street between rambling cottages. Other Norwood period canvases include a view of Charles Barry junior's newly-completed buildings for Dulwich College, two views of the Crystal Palace, *Snow at Lower Norwood* and a semi-rural panorama *Near Sydenham Hill.*

The works of the two French artists, exhibited in New Bond Street by their compatriot, the dealer Durand-Ruel, puzzled the English critics, although the relationship between the artists and the dealer was to remain crucial for the later success of them all. Pissarro longed to return to his home, even though he knew from friends that it was a ruin, as a letter to his friend Duret makes clear: "I am here for only a very short time. I count on returning to France as soon as possible ... it is only abroad that one feels how beautiful, great and hospitable France is. What a difference here! One gathers only contempt, indifference, even rudeness ... Here there is no art, everything is a question of business... My painting doesn't catch on, not at all.... "This last complaint was less than fair; it hadn't caught on in France so far either – hence the mountain of unsold canvases left for the Prussians to abuse.

From 1883 onwards Pissarro's son, Lucien, was mainly based in the bohemian colony of Bedford Park and, returning periodically to visit him, Pissarro *père* painted the sort of subjects Monet had favoured – the Thames, Hyde Park and Kew – but, despite their more acceptable subject-matter and greater English familiarity with Impressionism, these later works, like their predecessors of 1870-71 found their main market in Paris rather than London.

YOSHIO MARKINO

Yoshio Makino (1869-1956) lived in London for more than forty years and from 1928 to 1949 was celebrated enough to be listed in *Who's Who*, under the anglicised form of his surname, Markino. He had left Japan at the age of 24, determined to see the world and become an artist. Racism made his life wretched in California and the French language did for him in Paris, so at the age of 27 he finally pitched up in London, penniless. A kindly Naval Attaché at the Japanese Embassy took Markino under his wing, paying him out of his own pocket to do secretarial work so that he could attend art classes in the evenings. But when he was no longer needed at the Embassy Markino was forced to survive as best he could by selling illustrations and modelling at Goldsmith's College. Salvation came unexpectedly in the shape of an offer of employment by a monumental mason near Norwood Cemetery. Markino found cheap lodgings at No. 1 Martell Road, West Dulwich. He described the family as "simple and good-hearted, if rough", the landlady in particular being ill-tempered but scrupulously honest. By day Markino worked tracing or making designs for tombstones, a task he found infinitely depressing. In the evenings he continued to practise sketching, copying illustrations from magazines, because they were evidently what would sell. On Sundays his treat was to stroll through Dulwich village and consume a packet of Ogden's cigarettes, each packet of which contained a picture of a famous actress, which he collected, later confessing that "It was the very beginning of my real appreciation of English beauties." Markino's Dulwich idyll proved all too brief. His employer decided that his designs for angels lacked masculinity: "For goodness sake, don't draw such big pectorals on his figure! .... my customers are complaining that your angels look more like ballet girls."

Two weeks notice was given. Markino was reduced literally to his last coppers, then miraculously sold two dozen designs to a publisher for twelve guineas – enough to keep him for some months. Prudently, he left West Dulwich for less salubrious but even cheaper surroundings in a Brixton boarding-house; but it was to be another eight years before success finally came to Markino when his autobiographical account of his struggles and near-starvation – *A Japanese Artist in London* – earned him £1,000 in less than six months. The book's quaint prose and gentle humour won wide praise, *The Times* praising it as "literature by virtue of its artlessness". Markino went on to become a popular illustrator and essayist until the Second World War disrupted his comfortable life forever. Repatriated to Japan in 1942 after an absence of almost fifty years, he died in great poverty in 1956. His charming autobiography was, however, republished in England in 1991 and includes a selection of his accomplished water-colours of London street scenes, his favourite subject.

JAMES FITTON

Oldham-born James Fitton (1899-1982) moved into Pond Cottages, Dulwich in 1928 and lived there for the rest of his life. Trained at London's Central School, Fitton worked as a freelance commercial artist before becoming the highly successful art director of an advertising agency, working for major corporate clients, such as London Transport. Leftist in sympathies, he was prominent in intellectual anti-fascist circles in the 1930s, producing savage satirical cartoons in the style of his German contemporary George Grosz.

Over the course of his career Fitton exhibited some 170 canvases at the Royal Academy's Summer exhibitions, many of his oil paintings focusing on subjects drawn from the stage, circus and café life, which so appealed to his contemporaries like Sickert and other members of the London Group. Fitton also played an influential role in the development of design education in the UK and, despite his reputation as an irreverent *enfant terrible*, served on many governing bodies, including those of Dulwich Picture Gallery and the Camberwell School of Arts and Crafts.

A Dulwich amateur of a slightly older generation, Charles Core (1881-1947), claimed to have submitted over 150 paintings to the Royal Academy – and to have received more rejections than any other living artist.

THE SOUTH LONDON GALLERY

In 1868 William Rossiter established the South London Working Men's College in Blackfriars Road, enhancing its facilities with a free library and art gallery of paintings loaned by artists. After several moves, this pioneering institution relocated in 1887 to a warehouse at 207 Camberwell Road. Under the chairmanship of Lord Leighton, President of the Royal Academy, and with the support of the artist Sir Edward Burne-Jones and the eminent actor, Sir Henry Irving, a Council raised funds to erect the South London Fine Art Gallery in Peckham Road. Opened in 1891, it asserted its mission to bring art to the people by opening on Sundays, the only day most working folk had free, and by welcoming children, who were supplied with drawing materials and picture books to look at. Paintings were donated by such leading artistic figures as Val Prinsep and G.F. Watts. Other works in the collection now include, appropriately enough, water-colours by Paul (1725-1809) and Thomas Sandby (1721-1798), relatives of George Sandby, who was vicar of St Giles from 1795 to 1811, and paintings by society portraitist Sir Gerald Kelly R.A. (1879-1972), who was the son of a later vicar.

THE CAMBERWELL SCHOOL OF ARTS AND CRAFTS

Most of the funds for the erection of the South London Gallery were supplied by philanthropist, John Passmore Edwards (1823-1911), who was also the benefactor of public libraries at North Camberwell, Dulwich and Nunhead. Passmore Edwards, a self-

58. Peckham Road at the beginning of this century. The South London Art Gallery is on the left, and Camden Church (bombed in the last war) is in the centre.

made man, was a doughty supporter of progressive and sometimes unpopular causes, outspokenly opposing capital and corporal punishment and both the Crimean and Boer wars. He *twice* declined a knighthood offered in recognition of his generosity. In 1893 he funded the building of a lecture hall and museum extension at the rear of the new Gallery and then financed the construction next door of what was initially known as the Passmore Edwards Polytechnic Institute. When Camberwell Borough Council came into existence in 1900 it did so as the first local authority in the metropolis to have its own art gallery, museum and college of art.

The College passed to London County Council control in 1904, when the L.C.C. took over educational provision throughout the metropolis. The initial prospectus of the College proclaimed its primary purpose as being to "improve the skills of craftsmen" by providing "instruction in those branches of design and manipulation which directly bear on the more artistic trades"; but it soon extended its coverage to include fine arts training as well. True to its original objective, however, it is also noted for special expertise in such fields as ceramics, silversmithing and paper conservation.

The Sage of Denmark Hill

John Ruskin (1819-1900) is, like William Blake and William Morris, one of that select band who figure with equal prominence in the *Oxford Companion to Art* and the *Oxford Companion to English Literature*. The austere John Stuart Mill, author of standard texts on economics, politics, ethics and logic, considered Ruskin the only original thinker of his day – apart, of course, from himself. The historian G.M. Young, author of the magisterial *Victorian England: Portrait of an Age*, praised Ruskin's intellect as being "as profound, penetrating and subtle as any that England has seen" but conceded that he was also "endowed with every gift except the gift to organize the others." Ruskin himself was not unaware of this shortcoming, noting in his Inaugural Address at the Cambridge School of Art in 1858, "I am never satisfied that I have handled a subject properly till I have contradicted myself at least three times."

John Ruskin was born in Bloomsbury, the son of privilege and only child of a prospering wine-merchant and a doting, pious mother. Together they encouraged their offspring's intellectual precocity with indulgence and delight. In 1823, when Ruskin was just four, the family moved to a four-storied, semi-detached villa at 28 Herne Hill, which, in Ruskin's own words "commanded, in those comparatively smokeless days, a very notable view from its garret windows of the Norwood hills on one side and the winter sunrise over them; and of the valley of the Thames on the other, with Windsor telescopically clear in the distance, and Harrow, conspicuous always in fine weather to open vision against the summer sunset.' Even in old age Ruskin would regard this house as his *real* home and his childhood nursery as *his* room.

In 1842, just as Ruskin was completing his stint at Oxford, the family moved to a detached house, in much larger grounds, at 163 Denmark Hill, less than a mile away, with fine views over open countryside, as yet unsullied by suburban development. The lease on the Herne Hill house was, however, retained by the Ruskins after their move and, despite being sublet, was partly used to store Ruskin's collection of mineral specimens "out of the way of the tidiness of his mother's household." .

Educated largely at home, Ruskin gained from his parents a good grounding in the Bible and English literature and developed an early interest in the study of nature and in landscape painting. These interests were extended by childhood visits to the Lake Dis-

59. John Ruskin, from a photograph by Barraud.

trict and teenage travels on the continent, complemented by constant visits to Dulwich Picture Gallery, of which the *Encyclopaedia Britannica* observes unequivocally that "the pictures exhibited there remained the basis of his thoughts on art." Even before going up to Christ Church, Oxford in 1836 Ruskin began his literary career by contributing essays to the architectural and natural history publications edited by John Claudius Loudon.

Throughout his Oxford years (1836-42) Ruskin continued to travel in France, the Alps and Italy, while writing on architecture, composing poems in the manner of Byron and contributing to *Friendship's Offering*, which was edited by his friend and "literary godfather", W.H. Harrison. He also developed his considerable skills as a draughtsman and won the Newdigate Prize for poetry. But, like William Morris a decade later, Ruskin found the actual teaching at Oxford dreary and unprofitable and took a poor degree.

The first volume of *Modern Painters*, the work that established Ruskin as the foremost art critic of his age, appeared the year after he came down from Oxford, when he was just twenty-four. Ruskin's self-imposed task was to defend the work of contemporary landscape artists, especially Turner, and to demonstrate their "Superiority in the Art of Landscape Painting to all the Ancient Masters Proved by Examples of the True, the Beautiful and the Intellectual." Turner, accused by critics of 'defying' Nature, was, Ruskin asserted contrarily, the first painter in all history to have given "an entire transcript of the whole system of nature." Ruskin roundly condemned dutiful academic imitation of the seventeenth century masters and praised instead direct observation of the facts of nature. Volume II of *Modern Painters* (1846) more or less stands this argument on its head. Whereas Volume I was inspired by personal knowledge of practising artists who were also his friends, Volume II was based on an intensive study of medieval and renaissance sculpture, painting and architecture, chiefly in Italy. Belying its title, Volume II turned out to be an exaltation of "great men of old time."

Ruskin's Italian interlude awakened him to the dangers threatening Europe's architectural heritage – from ignorant neglect to revolutionary destruction, from industrial pollution to well-meaning 'restoration'. Diverting from the theme of natural beauty and its representation, to which he was to return in later volumes of *Modern Painters* (1856 and 1860), he produced *The Seven Lamps of Architecture* (1849) and *The Stones of Venice* (3 vols 1851-3). In the former Ruskin reminded his readers that "the most beautiful things in the world are the most useless; peacocks and lilies for instance" and urged that "when we build, let us think we build for ever." Ruskin's chapter "On the Nature of Gothic" in Volume II of *The Stones of Venice* came as a revelation to the young William Morris, then an undergraduate at Oxford, and served as the primary inspiration from which the Arts and Crafts movement subsequently developed. In this seminal essay Ruskin argued that the beauty of the Gothic style arose from the moral purity of the medieval social order in which the craftsman's work is joyful and creative, whereas the contemporary industrial order, corrupted and corroded by an ethic of plunder for profit, reduced work to mere labour, exploitative, alienating and incapable of creating true beauty. As the gospel of the Arts and Crafts movement, this assertion became the root of its emphasis on the skills and status of the craftsman, as well as its fascination with pseudo-medieval 'guilds' and 'brotherhoods '.

Ruskin's intellectual precocity was unmatched by his emotional development. At seventeen he had developed a passion for Adele Domecq, the daughter of his father's Spanish business partner. It came to nothing but left him scarred. At Oxford Ruskin's social life was constrained by the proximity of his anxious mother, who insisted on taking lodgings near his college. The onset of a haemorrhage in 1840, diagnosed as potentially consumptive, forced him to

winter in Italy and doubtless confirmed his mother's fears for his frailty and vulnerability. By 1845, however, researching in preparation for the second volume of *Modern Painters*, Ruskin was able to visit the Continent without his parents, albeit still accompanied by a personal valet. A return journey in 1846, to show his parents the natural and artistic beauties he had discovered, proved an anticlimax, provoking a bout of depression and lassitude.

Egged on by his concerned parents, Ruskin became engaged to Euphemia (Effie) Chalmers Grey, the vivacious daughter of Scottish family friends. They married in April 1848 and moved briefly into 30 Herne Hill but there was no meeting of minds – or bodies. The marriage was never consummated. Effie eventually fell in love with John Everett Millais, a member of the avant-garde clique who styled themselves the Pre-Raphaelite Brotherhood and whose work Ruskin had stoutly defended from hostile critics. As soon as Millais was elected to the Royal Academy and his professional future thereby assured, Effie deserted Ruskin, secured an annulment of their marriage in July 1854 and married Millais a few months later. He went on to acquire a baronetcy, a huge fortune and the Presidency of the Royal Academy.

Ruskin had never enjoyed Effie's attempts to drag him into London society and returned wounded, but doubtless also relieved, to the relative solitude of life at Denmark Hill. His isolation was periodically relieved by forays up to London to teach a drawing class at the Working Men's College in Queen Square, Bloomsbury or to sit at the feet of the historian Thomas Carlyle at his home in Cheyne Row, Chelsea. Carlyle reciprocated by riding over to Denmark Hill on his horse Fritz. Other visitors included, among writers Charles Kingsley, Henry James, Lord Tennyson and the historian J.A. Froude and among artists Turner, G.F. Watts, William Morris, Burne-Jones, Holman Hunt and (Sir) Hubert von Herkomer, who was to paint a portrait of Ruskin, posing in the Herne Hill room he had occupied as a child.

Ruskin's major literary focus was now the composition of the third and fourth volumes of *Modern Painters*, whose tone became increasingly declamatory and eccentric – viz. "Mountains are the beginning and the end of all natural scenery." His other preoccupations included advising on the building of the Oxford Museum of Natural History, which embodied his own theories about Gothic architecture, and the immense task of sorting and arranging the 20,000 drawings which Turner had bequeathed to the National Gallery. So unquestioned was Ruskin's status as an aesthetic arbiter that works which he considered 'unfinished', such as the 1843 version of *Norham Castle*, now proudly displayed in the Tate, were simply omitted from the catalogue and left to languish in storage until after his death.

Ruskin's failed marriage provided him with no emotional insights. When he professed his attachment to an unbalanced Irish teenager, picturesquely named Rose La Touche, her ultra-respectable parents were horrified; but his obsession with the girl endured, despite her mental and physical deterioration, and even after her death in 1875, haunting him in old age. Ruskin did, however, later find a periodic safe haven at the girls school run by Miss Bell at Winnington, Cheshire, where he could enjoy the innocence of female youth, unclouded by the taint of sexuality.

The death of Ruskin's father in 1864 left him possessed of numerous properties, a splendid collection of pictures and a huge fortune of £160,000. (William Morris, with an annual income of £900 was accounted a rich man.) Ruskin could afford to indulge his whims. Disliking railways intensely, he even designed his own coach, complete with his coat of arms on the doors, and had it built by a local firm, Tucker's of Camberwell, for the lordly sum of £190.

The death of Ruskin's father provoked no change in his daily routines and he continued to live quietly with his mother at Denmark Hill even after his election as the first Slade Professor of Fine Art at Oxford in 1869. Although his mannered style reminded one onlooker of "an elderly macaw picking grapes", Ruskin's Oxford lectures enjoyed great success. He generously donated to the university a large study collection of prints, drawings and photographs and founded a drawing school for the undergraduates. But he also maintained his interest in working-class self-improvement, writing exhortatory tracts in letter form and founding, with a capital of £10,000, the utopian Guild of St George to implement his idealistic economic doctrines; the most successful of its rather chaotic ventures was the establishment of a museum of art in Sheffield.

In 1997 the Ruskin gallery in Sheffield mounted an exhibition on 'Ruskin in Japan', which afforded a striking example of the impact of his writings in a country he never even visited. Ruskin's ideas affected not only Japanese art, literature and politics in the period of its rapid modernisation but also inspired movements to preserve or revive folk and peasant crafts. Even the sport of mountaineering in Japan owes a debt to him as founders of the Japan Alpine Club (1905) had been profoundly moved by his descriptions of mountain landscapes.

In 1871 Ruskin's mother died and in that same year he also suffered a severe bout of illness which kept him some weeks at Matlock. Added to these shocks were the all too visible changes taking place in Camberwell. Croxted Lane (now Road), where

Ruskin had wandered happily as a child was becoming a "deep-rutted cart-road, diverging into various pieces of waste, and bordered by heaps of everything unclean – ashes and rags, beer-bottles and old shoes, battered pans, smashed crockery, shreds of nameless clothes ... The lane now ends where its prettiest windings once began, being cut off by a cross-road leading out of Dulwich to a minor railway station, and what was of old the daintiest intricacy of its solitude is changed into a straight evenly macadamised carriage-way between new houses."

The traumas of bereavement and illness, added to his horror at the impact of the railways and speculative builders on the rural idyll he had known as a child, prompted Ruskin at last to quit Denmark Hill in favour of *Brantwood*, an ugly house with a beautiful view, looking out over Coniston Water in the Lake District. The Denmark Hill furniture was taken to furnish Ruskin's new home. Considering that Ruskin was one of the great aesthetic commentators of the century he appeared to many of his contemporaries to be generally indifferent to his domestic surroundings, most of his furnishings being inherited, hence rather old-fashioned, and seemingly jumbled together with little regard for harmonies of colour or scale. Nor, despite his growing distaste for Camberwell, could he let go of his old home emotionally: "I am happier than I was at Denmark Hill – and yet look back to Denmark Hill enraged at myself for not knowing its blessings."

The break with Camberwell was, however, less than absolute. Ruskin retained a fourteen year lease on 28 Herne Hill which he gave as a wedding-gift to his cousin and ward Joanna Agnew on her marriage to the artist Arthur Severn, the son of Keats' closest friend and companion, Joseph Severn. Ruskin considered that this gave him the right to use Herne Hill as a base whenever he needed to be in London. His old nursery became his study-bedroom – once the brass bedstead, to which he had taken an instant loathing, was disguised with chintz. He visited it for the last time on returning from the Continent in December 1888, staying there three weeks.

Neither communion with Nature nor the passage of the years brought Ruskin inner peace. After a severe bout of mental disorder in 1878, he resigned his professorship in 1879. Respite brought a temporary return to the lecture-platform but five more bouts of madness followed. Although for a while Ruskin continued to keep the diary he had begun at the age of 14, consolidating his memories into an autobiography, *Praeterita* (1885-9), for the last decade of his life the man whose collected works filled 39 volumes was incapable of writing anything more than his signature.

60. *Rural Idyll – a Camberwell thatched cottage at the end of the last century.*

The Early Suburb

COMMUTING AND COMMUNITY

The process of suburbanisation was directly linked with the development of transport systems, as contemporaries clearly recognised. In *London in 1850-1851* J.R. McCulloch characterised South London as the *locus classicus* of this phenomenon: "The picturesque hills of Surrey, near Dulwich and Norwood, are studded with the villas of citizens who retire there from the bustle of town ... This prevalent fashion among the Londoners of fixing their abode in the suburbs has been greatly encouraged by the easy communication afforded by the omnibuses and coaches which run to and from at all hours of the day, and till late at night."

Camberwell and Peckham were affected by this process far sooner and more profoundly than Dulwich. By 1841 Peckham with eleven residents per acre, and Camberwell with ten, already had local populations of quite a different order than Dulwich, which still had only one per acre. Twenty years later, just before railway penetration revolutionised the area, Peckham had twenty-four, Camberwell fifteen and Dulwich still only one.

A SUBURBAN ELITE

The list of subscribers to D.H. Allport's *Collections Illustrative of the Geology, History, Antiquities and Associations of Camberwell and the Neighbourhood* (1841) provides a cross-section of the area's social elite at that time. With the exception of the Denmark Place Chapel Book Society, all of the 139 named subscribers were individuals, eighteen of whom lived in other parts of London and ten of whom lived in other parts of England. Of the remaining 110, more than three-quarters styled themselves Esq., rather than Mr. The parish subscribers also included one M.D. and eleven Reverends, of whom the most distinguished was clearly the Rev. W.B. Collyer, the celebrated preacher of the Hanover Chapel, who had so many academic distinctions as to be listed as "D.D., LL.D., F.A.S. &c &c." – but even he was socially outranked by H.R.H. the Duke of Normandy.

Although Champion Lodge was only demolished in the year Allport's book was published, a Residents' Association, with thirteen members, representing the inhabitants of the estate built on its site, was already in existence by 1845. They may well have considered themselves something of an elite within the elite and were certainly affluent enough to employ their own full-time 'roadman' whose duties included street-cleaning, maintaining gravelled surfaces and drains,

61. Spring Mount, Denmark Hill – a detached villa of 1824. Note the laurels typical of the garden taste of that period.

tending to the gas-lighting and doubtless warning off any vagrants and urchins bold enough to approach the stout gates which protected their main thoroughfare from the insolent intrusions of through traffic. A minimum social tone was maintained on other newly-building estates by restrictive clauses in the building-leases which forbade the exercise of such environmentally offensive trades as those of the tallow-chandler, soapmaker, distiller, slaughterman or butcher.

A further measure of social exclusiveness was conferred on Camberwell by the residence of local notables, such as the artists David Cox, Samuel Prout and Henry Gastineau (see p55). The poet and journalist, Thomas Hood, lived at 181 and then 266 Camberwell New Road. George Grote (1794-1871) lived in Dulwich from 1832 to 1836. Having made his fortune in banking, he was relatively free to devote himself to scholarship and public service. A founder of the University of London, M.P. and Fellow of the Royal Society, Grote is chiefly remembered as the author of a magisterial eight-volume *History of Greece*, which won him a memorial in Poets' Corner.

Another indicator of the good standing of the locality was the birth, to families of comfortable but relatively obscure circumstances, of individuals who would achieve national fame in the future. The poet Robert Browning was born in 1812 at Rainbow

62. A fine early Victorian terrace in Havil Street.

63. *The variety of styles in Addington Square implies development in stages by separate, small-scale developers.*

64. *Camberwell Grove 1836. The elegant clothes of mother and child denote the social standing of the anticipated residents of these new villas.*

65. A former keeper's lodge, from which visitors to Grove Park could be discreetly evaluated. It has since been enlarged to make a modest dwelling.

66. The poet and journalist, Thomas Hood, who lived at 181 and then 266 Camberwell New Road.

Cottage, Cottage Green, Southampton Way and the Liberal politician Joseph Chamberlain was born in 1836 at 88 Camberwell Grove. Browning's father was a Bank of England official, who owned a piano, a library of 6,000 books and a back garden big enough to stable a pony for his son. Both Browning and Chamberlain received their early education locally. Browning's classmates included Joseph Arnould, a future head of the Supreme Court in Bombay and Alfred Domett, Prime Minister of New Zealand in 1862-1863. Another locally-born luminary was the reforming Master of Balliol College, Oxford, Benjamin Jowett (1817-1893) whose apparent omniscience inspired the mocking squib:

> "First come I;
> My name is Jowett,
> There's no knowledge, but I know it.
> I am Master of this College,
> What I don't know isn't knowledge."

67. *The historian, George Grote, a Dulwich resident from 1832 to 1836.*

68. *The birthplace of Joseph Chamberlain MP, at 88 Camberwell Grove.*

69. *Robert Browning, born in Rainbow Cottage, Southampton Way. Photograph by W.H. Grove.*

70. *Joseph Chamberlain MP, drawing by Phil May.*

71. Sir Henry Bessemer's house. Bessemer's perfection of a process for mass-producing steel in 1859 made him a millionaire and a Fellow of the Royal Society. His 114 patents included the perforated die-stamp, a type-composing machine, improved techniques for sugar refining and manufacturing bronze powder, and imitation velvet. Six towns in the USA were named after him.

72. The dining room of Bessemer's house.

73. Camberwell Grove nowadays – cars have replaced carriages.

ENTREPRENEURS AND EXILES

One peculiarity of the Camberwell bourgeoisie was the presence of a substantial German community of some eighty families, most of whom derived their wealth from commercial or financial business in the City of London. The Old Burial ground in Dulwich Village is the last resting-place of one of their earlier representatives, Louisa Schroder, who died in 1824. The epicentre of their existence was Denmark Hill – "the Belgravia of South London" – and their presence explains the local establishment of a German delicatessen, a Camberwell German Choir and even a German undertaker. In 1855 they opened their own Evangelical church in Windsor Road, with seating for three hundred persons. In that same year a prominent member of the community and keen patron of the arts, Herr Beneke, who had entertained Mendelssohn, extended his hospitality to Richard Wagner, then visiting London in his capacity as a conductor. Rather less publicity, one assumes, attended the simultaneous sojourn of Karl Marx and his family, who temporarily fled their Soho garret to escape creditors and were offered refuge in Camberwell by ex-teacher and fellow-revolutionary Peter Imandt. Marx and Imandt subsequently revealed that another local resident, passing himself off as Charles Fleury, a businessman, was in fact a Prussian agent.

On the whole a German spy should have had an easy time of it. Although German political exiles, such as the distinguished art historian and poet Gottfried Kinkel (1815-82), were occasionally invited to Camberwell to lecture, the community as such remained apolitical, ultra-respectable and firmly supportive of the institutions of their adopted country. They did not, however, neglect their cultural heritage and on 10 November 1859 assembled at the Crystal Palace to celebrate the centenary of the birth of Schiller in the shadow of an immense bust of the dramatist sculpted by Andreas Grass.

A speech by the eloquent Kinkel was followed by the singing of a Schiller poem set to music by local resident Ernst Pauer and the proceedings then closed with a torchlight procession.

The existence of the Camberwell German community is commemorated in the name of Frankfurt Road, adopted from Frankfurt Villa. At 105 Denmark Hill, once the home of one Fritz Rommel, the name 'Osnabruck' was for long just discernible on the gatepost. He was living there in 1888. In 1892 the merchant banker Herman Kleinworth, founder of Kleinwort Benson, moved into the magnificent residence which he styled The Platanes, from the German name for the plane trees which still shade the front garden.

After he moved out he donated it to King's College, to serve as a student hostel.

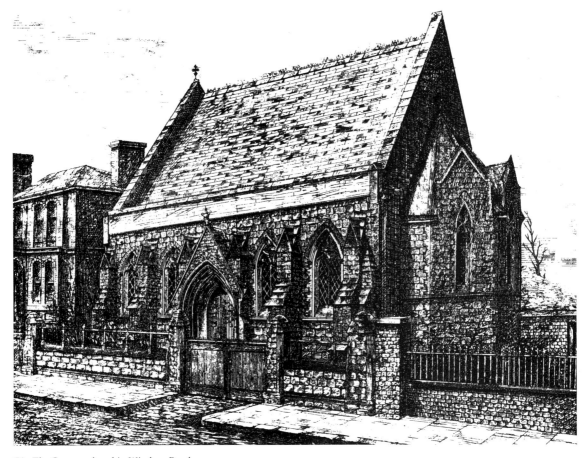

74. *The German chapel in Windsor Road.*

75. *The Platanes, former residence of the Kleinworth family on Champion Hill.*

INSTITUTIONAL LIVING

Camberwell's still leafy environment and reputation for salubriousness doubtless influenced the several charitable bodies which chose to buy or build residential facilities for the elderly, infirm or distressed in the growing suburb. Peckham House, an eighteenth-century mansion formerly occupied by the Spitta family, was converted into a private mental home in 1826 and continued to function as such until 1951. What had once been Alfred House School, and then briefly the Royal Naval School, was from 1846 to 1954, the Camberwell House Asylum. The Friendly Female Asylum, erected in Gloucester Place by voluntary contributions in 1821, proclaimed on a tablet its modest function as a refuge for "aged persons who have seen better days". Far more splendid was the Licensed Victuallers' Benevolent Institution, which gave its name to Asylum Road, in which it still stands. Hailed in Prof. Pevsner's *The Buildings of England* as "the only grand composition amongst the many almshouses of Camberwell", it was designed by Henry

76. The Licensed Victuallers' Asylum in Asylum Road.

Rose, architect of the later Licensed Victuallers' School in Kennington Lane, Lambeth and was built between 1827 and 1833 in a style Pevsner characterises as "frugally detailed classical." The Licensed Victuallers enjoyed royal patronage, the foundation stone being laid by H.R.H. the Duke of Sussex "with full Masonic honours". A 'Ladies Wing' was added to the building in 1849 (foundation stone courtesy of H.R.H. Albert, the Prince Consort), and further ranges in 1858, 1862 and 1866, until the complex eventually contained 176 dwellings, housing over two hundred inmates, who received not only "pecuniary assistance" but also free coal and medical treatment. Inspired by this example the Metropolitan Beer and Wine Trade Society, established in 1834 as an organisation parallel to the Licensed Victuallers, erected their own almshouses at Nunhead in 1851.

Parliament's passage of a rigorous, not to say punitive, 'New Poor Law' in 1834 may have provoked the outburst of charitable construction which gave Camberwell three new similar institutions. It also prompted the creation, by members of the Hill Street Chapel, of a Peckham Pension Society and by the Rev. Edmund Lilley of St Chrysostom's of the Peckham and Kent Road Pension Society. These were expressly intended to keep former ratepayers from the un-tender mercies of the new workhouses, where they would be offered but the barest subsistence in the harshest of circumstances. In 1834 a City of London livery company, the Girdlers, were responsible for erecting a pseudo-Tudor home in Consort Road, known as Beeston's Gift in memory of the charitable fund bequeathed by Cuthbert Beeston, a

77. Beeston's Gift, the Girdlers' Company almshouses in Consort Road.

member of the company, who had died in 1582. In 1851 the Girdlers built another range of almshouses in Choumert Road. In Westmoreland Place, Southampton Street, the Aged Pilgrims' Society put up almshouses (1837) around a turfed quadrangle; these were described by Allport as "exceedingly neat and picturesque". The forty-two resident 'Pilgrims' were simply "aged Christians, whose consistent character forms the only required claim to admission"; the same charity also supported over three hundred 'out-pensioners'. The site of the Pilgrims' home was donated by one William Peacock, who in 1838 also established a Bethel asylum in Havil Street for "twelve aged women". One other institution also mentioned by Allport was "a nunnery said to belong

78. The Aged Pilgrims' Home in Camberwell.

79. Bethel Asylum in Havil Street.

to the order of St. Bridget" which for some years occupied a large residence in Meeting House Lane, Peckham until "the inmates ... decamped in the night, without previous notice, defrauding the good tradespeople of Peckham to a considerable amount." The same author hinted at further dark doings in recording a rumour that "several of the nuns lie buried in the garden, but no memorials exist."

A PLACE OF PLEASURE

Despite its rapid growth in population and consequent urbanisation, the Camberwell area continued until mid-century to serve as a resort for pleasure-seekers from the metropolis. Peckham Fair was abolished in 1827 following the advent of the Grand Surrey Canal and the urbanisation of its environs but Camberwell Fair continued to be held on semi-rural Camberwell Green for another generation (see ills 31 and 81). Its attractions included Richardson's travelling theatre and Wombwell's famous menagerie, as well as bands, side-shows and stalls proffering the dubious delights of oysters and even more questionable sausages and pies. The rising tide of respectability which accompanied the accession of Queen Victoria led local residents to resent the annual invasion of "nomadic thieves, coarse men and lewd women" which accompanied the traditional three days of festivity running up to St Giles' Day, on

1 September. The Vestry, moreover, resented the expense of hiring in police to supervise the occasion. In 1855 the Fair was finally abolished for good.

Another attraction which, according to its historian, "had a brief but lively existence from 1849 till about 1857", was Flora Gardens, which stood on Wyndham Road. Here "a central walk, adorned with fountains and lawns on either hand, led to a ballroom on the right, and on the left to a maze in the middle of which" it also had a "magic hermitage inhabited by a learned Chaldean astrologer." Sixpence secured admission to this demi-paradise any summer's evening, when concerts and dancing were nightly organised. In 1851 Flora Gardens was taken over by James Ellis, who had formerly leased the much larger and more famous Cremorne Gardens until going bankrupt in 1849. Bouncing back with style, Ellis put on a series of extravaganzas which included a balloon ascent, an eighteenth-century French costume ball, an 'Arabian Nights' entertainment, a mock-election and a three day '1,000 Guineas Fete', which featured a steeplechase by lady jockeys and a torchlight procession honouring Lady Godiva. Whatever inconveniences these junketings may have imposed on local residents, they were no doubt partly assuaged by the management's policy of opening the Gardens free on Sundays. Their hour of glory was, however, brief and by 1863 the site had been covered with new houses.

80. Friern Manor Dairy Farm in Peckham was a well-known supplier of milk to the metropolis. It was featured in the Illustrated London News in June 1853 in an article which extolled the quantity of milk that the cows yielded – between 20 and 24 quarts a day. The sheds were lit by gas so that night milking could take place. Fourteen milkers were employed, all of whom were "of the rougher sex".

81. *Camberwell Fair c.1850, on the eve of its suppression. The proceedings have become much more commercialised and the dancing male figures in the middle imply much consumption of alcohol.*

SUBURBAN PARADISE

To the newcomer during that early phase of suburbanisation a well-laid garden, though it might be negligible in scale compared with the magnificence of Bond's imitation Versailles, was an essential symbol of his status and achievement. As Charles Dickens himself mischievously observed "If the regular City man ... can be said to have any daily recreation beyond his dinner it is his garden. He never does anything to it with his own hands; but he takes great pride in it notwithstanding ... He always takes a walk round it, before he starts for town in the morning, and is particularly anxious that the fish-pond should be kept specially neat ... his delight in his garden appears to arise more from the consciousness of possession than actual enjoyment of it. When he drives you down to dinner on a weekday ... he orders the French windows of his dining-room (which of course look into the garden) to be opened, and ... descants at considerable length upon its beauty, and the cost of maintaining it." (*Sketches by Boz*)

This was, perhaps, less than entirely fair. The green murmurings of a garden also represented the antithesis of the most characteristic features of the City of London – clangorous noise and smoky pollution. It was not only an icon but a refuge for the City man, as Dickens himself also conceded: "If you call on him on Sunday in summer-time, about an hour before dinner, you will find him sitting in an arm-chair, on the lawn behind the house, with a straw hat on, reading a Sunday paper."

Fashion also came into it. The suburban cult of gardening was decisively advanced at this very time by the publication of England's first popular horticultural journal, the *Gardener's Magazine* (1826), edited by John Claudius Loudon. Loudon proclaimed quite openly that one of the major purposes of a garden was "to display the taste and wealth of the possessor." In 1838 he published what became a standard handbook for the horticulturally ambitious, *The Suburban Gardener and Villa Companion*.

The generously-spaced houses being built in Camberwell afforded ample scope for Loudon's disciples. He advocated the replacement of the sombre yews and dreary conifers, which then dominated London squares, with sycamores, planes or almond trees. Interestingly, John Ruskin, who as a teenager had contributed to another of Loudon's publications – Britain's first architectural journal – entitled a memoir of his first home *Almond Blossoms at Herne Hill*. More typically, suburban front gardens, screened by a substantial brick wall, sported a patch of grass lawn and a gravel driveway, flanked and shaded by ornamental bushes and trees such as laurels, limes and laburnums. Rear gardens had flower beds and, usually a range of fruit trees and bushes to produce apples, pears, plums, currants and gooseberries to be eaten in season, turned into jams or pickles and given to neighbours and callers. Flower beds were increasingly given over to bedding-plants, raised in greenhouses and planted out *en bloc* – a fashion imported from China. Complex rules were promulgated to guide the shapes of the beds and the combinations of colours to be planted next to each other.

Although the ladies of the house might cut flowers for arranging in the house, serious garden work was relegated to professionals. John Ruskin's father had a front garden with a landmark cedar and a rear garden of over three acres, which included a kitchen garden, an orchard and a 'woodwalk'. There was also a meadow, equally large, with a stable, a pigsty and three cows providing milk, cream and butter for the household. Four men were employed maintaining this miniature estate. Loudon would certainly have approved, having argued that "every man who does not limit the vegetable part of his dinner to bread and potatoes is a patron of gardening, by creating a demand for its production. The more valuable patrons are those who regularly have dessert on their tables after dinner, or who maintain throughout the year beautiful nosegays and pots of flowers in their lobbies and drawing-rooms." Ruskin himself increased the number of gardeners to seven and routinely presented female visitors with a bouquet of flowers to take away with them. "The camellias and azaleas stand in the anteroom of my library," he noted with pleasure, "and my young lady friends have leave to gather what they like to put in their hair, when they are going to balls."

Technology, trade and territorial expansion combined to change the grander suburban gardens as the century advanced. The invention of the lawnmower in the 1830s encouraged householders to lay down more of their gardens to grass. Loudon's invention of curved glazing bars encouraged the building of stylish hothouses and conservatories in which to grow exotic and novel plants from the farthest reaches of the empire on which the sun never set – palms from West Africa and decorative ferns from remote New Zealand. Gardens themselves were further brightened with azaleas from China and rhododendrons from the foothills of the Himalayas.

The ghosts of such plantings can still be detected along the southern and eastern edges of Dulwich Upper Wood, where the Victorian villas of the 1860s had been demolished by the 1960s. Here rhododendrons, cherry laurels, cedar of Lebanon and even a monkey puzzle tree do battle against invading native species, such as sycamore and blackberry, as they recolonise their ancient home, threatening to overrun a disused tennis lawn in the south-east corner of the wood and engulf a pseudo-Gothic folly near its heart.

82. *Itinerant tradesmen were an important part of daily lives. This picture shows a costermonger selling firewood, and chopping it up on site.*

STREET LIFE

A.R. Bennett, the author of *London and Londoners in the Eighteen-Fifties and Sixties* (1924), lived in Camberwell from 1855 to 1860. His memoirs bring back a neighbourhood which, on the eve of the railway age, retained the vestiges of its connections with the countryside. As a young child pretty much confined to the house, Bennett particularly recalled the characters, sights and sounds which spasmodically enlivened the subdued atmosphere of quietly respectable residential streets. Officialdom was represented by policemen, who still wore tall leather hats and carried rattles rather than whistles, and, more colourfully, by postmen, ablaze in scarlet coats bright with buttons. But these were rare intruders.

Far more frequent disturbers of domestic tranquility were nomadic traders. Some passed by daily – milkmen dressed in country smocks and carrying their pails from a yoke, potmen from local public houses, bringing round ale, porter and stout, and butchers' boys calling early to take orders for meat to be delivered in time for cooking the same day. Once or twice a week there was the muffin man, ringing his bell and carrying a tray of cakes and crumpets, or girls crying fresh watercress or lavender or a costermonger, pushing a barrow of fresh vegetables. Selling meat for cats and groundsel for canaries were separate and distinctive trades. Some items were sold only seasonally. In spring householders were offered fly-traps and paper ornaments to disguise the ugly void of a fire-less grate. Summer brought vendors of cherries and strawberries. In autumn hawkers came round with sawdust-filled draught-excluders for ill-fitting doors and windows. Other trades were associated with the maintenance of the houses and the streets themselves – sooty sweeps, sharpeners of knives, menders of cane- and rush-bottomed chairs and drivers of water-carts to lay the summer dust on roads not yet macadamised. Servants made a few pennies on the side by selling cast-off clothes and broken household items to Jewish dealers and bought the tools of their trade – brooms and brushes and pegs and clothes-props – from itinerant gypsies.

Scavengers with horse-drawn carts plied the streets, ringing a hand-bell to attract attention. Their income

83. *Workers on the Grove Park Dairy Farm, 1860.*

came from re-cycling or re-selling what they collected. Cinders went to make bricks, rags to make paper, paper to make cardboard, bones to make glue, kitchen-waste to feed pigs. Whatever could not readily be re-cycled or re-sold usually required the disbursement of coppers or ale to be got rid of.

Looking back from the vantage-point of the 1920s Bennett concisely summarised the forces which rapidly eroded the street panorama of his Camberwell infancy: "improved mechanical appliances, transport and distribution facilities – stricter police regulations – stringent pedlars' licences – concentration of trade by large firms" – changes epitomised or complemented by the rise of the suburban High Street. In Camberwell such a phenomenon was still embryonic in 1860, but *Kelly's Street Directory* for that year already lists more than 300 food shops and some twenty dairies, plus seventy retailers of beer, not including public houses. Clothing could be supplied or repaired by fifty makers of boots and shoes, thirty-odd tailors and more than twenty each of milliners and drapers. The other most plentiful retail outlets were tobacconists and chemists, each numbering over twenty. There was also a specialised seller of sheet-music and even, to pander to parental pride and personal vanity, a single 'photographist'.

The Railway Suburb

" The richest crop for any field
Is a crop of bricks for it to yield
The richest crop that it can grow,
Is a crop of houses in a row."
Tarbuck's *Handbook of House Property* (1875)

As early as 1846 the *Report of the Royal Commission on Railway Termini within or in the immediate vicinity of the Metropolis* noted acutely that:

" ... those parts of Surrey and Kent which are within a short distance of London are generally more thickly inhabited by persons having occupations in London, and are more frequented for occasional relaxation than the corresponding parts of Essex, Middlesex and Hertfordshire."

A leading modern scholar, considering this trend in retrospect, came to an unflattering conclusion about its impact:

"the improvement of transport facilities often lowered the social tone of a neighbourhood, by making possible denser housing and commercial development. When, in 1863, Herne Hill became an important junction for the London, Chatham and Dover, from which trains left for both Victoria and the line to Blackfriars and Holborn Viaduct, the standing of the neighbourhood as a wealthy residential district was doomed. In 1866 a loop line joined Denmark Hill to both Victoria and London Bridge. Both communities were soon covered with streets of cheap houses."
(Donald G. Olsen – *The Growth of Victorian London* 1976)

A nation-wide analysis of rapid (i.e. 25%+) population growth in the decade 1871-81 has revealed that what in 1900 became the metropolitan borough of Camberwell was one of 23 English boroughs in this category. The building frenzy peaked in Camberwell between 1878 and 1880 when no less than 416 firms or individual builders were at work erecting 5,670 new houses in what the *Building News* politely described as "close-set nests of bricks and mortar." Inevitably not all could prosper. In 1881, of 4,800 houses recently built in East Dulwich some forty per cent remained untenanted, forcing speculators to offer rent reductions of ten to fifteen per cent.

THE RAILWAY COMES

As H.J. Dyos, the classic chronicler of suburbia, noted: "the locomotive was in truth practically middle-aged before it appeared in Camberwell." The first main line from London to Southampton passed several miles to the west, the line to Brighton and Dover to the east. In 1852 a new line to the Crystal Palace, relocated at Sydenham after the closure of the Great

84. Rural railway – once clear of Camberwell proper, commuters passed through substantial sections of green corridor.

85. Denmark Hill Station was opened in 1866 to become the most central of all commuting points in the area. Fired by vandals in 1980, it was threatened with closure until saved by the determined efforts of the Camberwell Society and re-opened in 1986 with its main booking-hall converted into a pub.

86. North Dulwich Station.

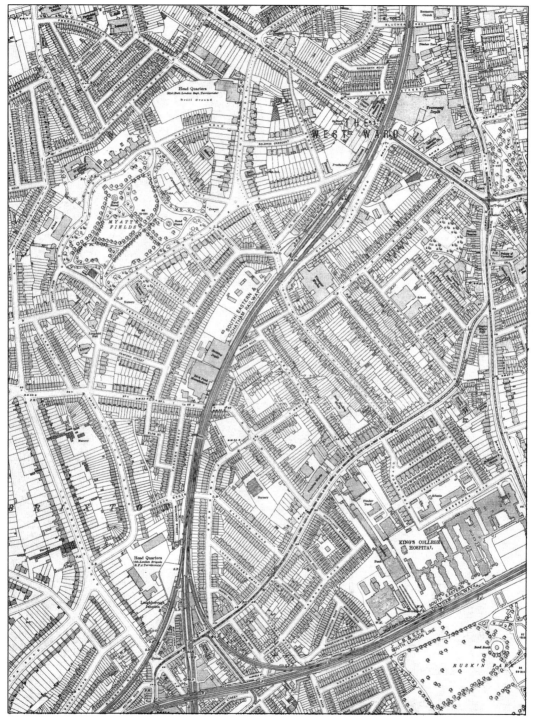

87. Camberwell in 1913, crossed by railways. Electrification came to the Camberwell area in 1909 and was hailed as a major boon to commuters. Journey times to London termini were cut by up to a third and fares substantially reduced. The new rolling-stock was also praised as far less draughty than what it replaced.

88. Heraldry of Steam – armorial bearings on the bridge at North Dulwich station invoke Edward Alleyn (right) and the communities served by the original railway company, including the City of London.

89. Engineer of Empire. The last resting place of James Berkeley (1819-62) occupies a commanding site in Camberwell Old Cemetery. Trained by Robert Stephenson himself, Berkeley was responsible for building the first railways in India. Admirers raised £3,000 to construct his imposing tomb.

Exhibition in Hyde Park, clipped the edge of the area, establishing stations at Streatham and Norwood. But it was another decade before the London, Chatham & Dover Railway – irreverently known as the 'Run Down, Smash'em and Roll Over' – opened its stations at Camberwell New Road and Herne Hill. In 1866 the same company co-operated with its rival, the London, Brighton & South Coast Railway, to finance a new line from London Bridge with stations at Old Kent Road, Queen's Road, Peckham Rye and Denmark Hill, running through eventually to East Brixton and terminating at Battersea. Shortly afterwards the South London & Sutton Junction Railway opened stations at Champion Hill (after 1888 known as East Dulwich) and North Dulwich.

SUBURBAN SURVEYS

Anyone contemplating moving to the capital a century or so ago would have found invaluable guidance in W. S. Clarke's *The Suburban Homes of London: A Residential Guide to Favourite London Localities, Their Society, Celebrities and Associations*". Over fifty chapters cover the burgeoning fringes of the metropolis, "combining hints social, religious, sanitary and financial."

Clarke brackets Camberwell and Peckham together, emphasising that "to those who know anything of the green slopes which used to meet the eye not so very long ago, nothing is more surprising than the mushroom-like growth of bricks and mortar in this particular district." The railway is singled out as the prime factor behind this transformation but given short shrift as a facility: "there is a good service of trains ... but the rolling-stock is not what it should be, while the stations are as a rule both inconvenient in construction and ill-placed ... the greatest portion of the traffic is carried on by means of the omnibuses and trams. Of these, fortunately, there are a good supply." The houses along Camberwell New Road, "a thoroughfare somewhat too regular to be artistic" are praised for their large gardens but the houses themselves are condescendingly characterised as "slightly old-fashioned", if "roomy and convenient." Even less desirable is "another specimen of old Camberwell ... whose glory has now departed" – the area lying south of the Peckham Road towards St George's Church. The houses, "built about the commencement of the stucco period", are disfigured by peeling paintwork or over-sized porticoes "and, judged by the aesthetic taste of today, must be termed somewhat barbarous." Camberwell Grove, however, retains "a comfortable old-world flavour, a suspicion of wealth, and considerably more than a suspicion of the picturesque." Other desirable areas singled out for praise include Brunswick Square, the thirty-acre De Crespigny Park Estate on Champion Hill and Denmark Hill "where houses become mansions and gardens grounds." Peckham, however, is all but dismissed with a back-handed compliment: "Whatever shortcomings Peckham may have, it certainly has the merit of being very accessible."

Dulwich, despite being in effect a dependency of Camberwell, is allocated more than twice as many pages, over half of them being devoted to the stories of Edward Alleyn and Dulwich College. The author's commendations of the locality itself amount to an almost unstinted eulogy: "summer and autumn walks of the richest and pleasantest kind ... [and] ... the incessant change of villa architecture placed in the most delightful curving roads ... make Dulwich of the present time more attractive than when Dickens in his happiest book placed his happiest man in the happiest locality, in Dulwich."

90. *A Tilling's horse bus draws up outside the great Jones & Higgins emporium in Rye Lane, Peckham. As the advertisements on the bus make clear, Tilling's ran several subidiary businesses, including a riding-school and carriage hire for weddings and excursions.*

91. *An electric tram dating from 1907, shortly after this new service penetrated the Camberwell area.*

92. *Suburban swank. This house at 197 Camberwell Grove was sufficiently grand for its owners to have commissioned their own postcard.*

Clarke's verdict was echoed a decade later by Percy Fitzgerald in his *London City Suburbs* (1893): "The air here seems ever mild and salubrious; there is an abundance of old trees by the roadside with pleasant fields stretching far away. There are gentle ascents by Denmark Hill and Redpost Hill. Here are comfortable-looking mansions of old-fashioned and formal cut that seem to doze on in tranquil fashion. The speculative builder has not, as yet, done much mischief ... The fair country seems to commence here, for the long, densely-crowded rows of town houses stop abruptly at Camberwell Green, whence there spread out at once the inviting rural roads to Sydenham and Dulwich."

The semi-rural nature of the southern half of the area may still have attracted up-market residents and the manufacturers of picture postcards; but modern scholarship has questioned whether, taken as a whole, Camberwell could still be considered even a suburb when it achieved borough status: "By 1900 it is far from certain whether the historian is dealing with a suburb or a veiled new town because many, perhaps a majority, of the occupied part of the population of 259,000 both lived and worked in

Camberwell itself." (P.J. Waller – *Town, City and Nation, England 1850-1914,* publ. 1983)

If the achievement of borough status was a recognition that Camberwell functioned as a largely self-contained urban community this did not necessarily imply that its inhabitants enjoyed a vibrant and varied communal existence. Writing in 1909, the distinguished London historian Sir Walter Besant damned the then suburbs for creating "as dull a life as mankind ever tolerated", burdened moreover with "... all the exclusiveness and class feeling of London with none of the advantages of a country town".

SERVANTS, CLERKS AND WORKERS

The economic structure of post-railway Camberwell was both distinctive and diverse. The greatest single employment category was domestic service, an overwhelmingly female occupation; in this respect the suburb mirrored the metropolis as a whole. After that came the largest concentration of clerks south of the Thames, roughly one in eight of all the clerical workers in the capital. Clerical work represented the main avenue of upward mobility from the labouring-classes into the ranks of what were then literally 'white collar' workers. Products of the new Board Schools, these clerks, overwhelmingly male, were minor cogs in the massive commercial machine which made London the world's busiest international port. An increasing proportion, however, would be finding positions with local employers, such as the Peckham Mutual Permanent Building Society, the South Metropolitan Gas Works or the local branch of the Metropolitan Water Board. It has been estimated that by the first decade of the present century some two-thirds of the new borough's working population was employed within its boundaries or those of its immediate neighbours.

Local employers whose names would have been known throughout the metropolis included Tillings bus company, which by 1905 had some 7,000 horses at its disposal, Samuel Jones, manufacturer of 'Butterfly' brand gummed paper and other stationery products, and R. White, maker of a leading brand of mineral water. The borough labour force also included a tenth of all London's printers and a seventh of its hat-makers. Other local specialisms included the manufacture of watches, umbrellas, gas mantles, perambulators, pickles, printing machinery, leather goods and false teeth. In the Peckham area alone could be found a brewery and factories making pianos, 'athletic goods', shirts and yeast. New occupations were represented by gas-fitters and dry-cleaners, older traditions by makers of stays and corsets, a pewterer, a carver and gilder, a maker of picture-frames and a herbalist.

93. *High-rise apartments in the 'Queen Anne' style built in 1900 by a philanthropic trust and intended for industrious aspirants to the lower middle-classes.*

94. *The crest of the Four per Cent Industrial Dwellings Company, which built Evelina Mansions above. The directors did not visualise the company as a charity, but one which would hope to give its shareholders at least four per cent on their investment.*

The presence of 'motor engineers' and several firms making bicycles signified a new era in personal mobility but horse-drawn vehicles still predominated and so there were still local wheelwrights, farriers and builders of coaches, vans and carts. The growth and turnover of commercial and residential properties in the borough created business for numerous firms of estate agents, auctioneers, solicitors, architects, house furnishers, linen drapers, signwriters, builders and decorators. A large, growing and socially ambitious lower middle-class provided clients for locally-based teachers of music, dancing, shorthand and the curriculum required by the examiners for the Civil Service.

It was all rather different in Dulwich village, where the local population consisted largely of *rentiers*, the retired or commuters to prestigious and well-paid positions in the city centre. The most important employment categories in the village were domestic service, gardening, education and retailing. Professional occupations were represented by five doctors (including a *female* surgeon), a solicitor, a barrister and a chartered accountant. Pet-keeping was, apparently, sufficiently common to provide a living for a veterinarian *and* a 'canine doctor'; there were no less than eight builders and decorators. The traditional economy of the parish was represented by three working farms, a saddler and a blacksmith. Other occupations included two boot-makers, a cycle-maker, a sign-writer and a monumental mason.

Shops and Pleasures

RETAILING REVOLUTION

The opening of the Jones & Higgins drapery stores at No. 3 Rye Lane in 1867 marked a major turning-point in Peckham's transformation into one of south London's leading shopping centres. By the following year the partners had expanded into No. 5 and by 1871 had taken over No. 7 as well. Seven more premises would be absorbed over the next ten years and by 1914 they would occupy Nos. 1 to 23, 37 to 41 and 45. The 1880s witnessed the advent of Henry Holdron's Market, a covered 'mini-mall' and, a rival to Jones & Higgins, the drapery firm of Ely Thomas, which eventually divided the Jones & Higgins empire, occupying Nos. 25 to 35. Multiple stores arrived over the following two decades – Lipton's (1891), the hatters Dunn & Co. and the Singer Sewing Machine Co. (1895), Freeman, Hardy & Willis (1904), Maypole Dairy and Boots (1907), Home & Colonial and J. Lyons (1910) and Stead & Simpson (1911).

These large businesses continued to co-exist with many small, competing outlets. In 1914, along the west side of Rye Lane alone there were thirteen tailors, eight boot and shoe shops, six tobacconists, four each of confectioners, butchers and hairdressers, three each of ironmongers, glass and china dealers, watch-makers, chemists and coal merchants, two each of photographers, fishmongers, newsagents and undertakers and a music seller, a florist and a dealer in "incandescent light fittings",

By 1911 the borough of Camberwell had over 3,500 shops – one for every seventy-five inhabitants. And of these some five hundred were lock-up premises, which denoted the growing trend in the service sector towards the separation of home and work which industrialisation had already brought to much manufacturing.

Camberwell retained a diverse industrial sector well into the middle of the present century. Printing continued to be a major employer, with no less than six local firms placing advertisements in the Council's 1950 Jubilee handbook. Other employers included trades associated with the printing industry, such as stationery, bookbinding and the manufacture of cardboard boxes and paper, and a range of metal-working manufacturers producing gates, perambulators, exhibition stands, scientific instruments, bicycles and bottle-tops. Food-processing businesses included bakeries and manufacturers of ice-cream, peanuts and soft drinks.

95. *Despite the rush of building and businesses in the area, these stables, reputed to be 300 years old, were still in business in 1904, when this postcard was published.*

96. *E. Messenger, oil and colorman in Peckham Grove, early this century.*

97. *A Dulwich estate agent which prospered in the building boom – Marten & Carnaby in Thurlow Park Road and at 119 Dulwich Village.*

98. *Samuel Earl, mangle repairer, c.1905.*

TIBBLES' DAIRY

Pure Milk and Cream, Butter and
New Laid Eggs
guaranteed from our own Farm.

99. Tibbles' Dairy at 11 High Street, Peckham.

JOSIAH MESSENT

Gentlemen's, Ladies' and
Boys' Tailor.

**Gents' Tailoring
Department.**

NEW & COMPLETE
RANGES of CLOTHS
ARE NOW READY
FOR INSPECTION.

Blue & Grey Mixtures,
Black & Grey Checks
and Mixed Heather
Tones.

☐

Lounge Suit from **45/-**

Raglan Overcoat (full
skirted) from - **42/-**

Morning Coat & Vest
from - - - - **39/6**

**To Measure.
Patterns on request.**

Open Saturdays and other
nights till **9** p.m.

THURSDAYS - - 1 o'clock

101. Josiah Messent, tailor at 57/59 Queen's Road, Peckham.

100. H. Buckeridge at 293 Walworth Road, with a typical butcher's display, c.1890.

102. *George Waller, men's outfitters, in Camberwell Church Street, c.1900.*

103. *Ye Olde Bun House, c.1895, at 96 Peckham High Street.*

THE DEMON DRINK

The 1870s witnessed average alcohol consumption per head reach its high point for the century as the price of bread and other foodstuffs fell significantly, thanks to railways and steamships which had opened up vast tracts of North America, Australia and Argentina to profitable cultivation. The result was greatly to enlarge the disposable incomes of the poor. Breweries were swift to mop up much of the new purchasing power. Traditional inns and taverns were complemented by flamboyant new 'gin-palaces'. These were, as Camberwell's local historian W.H. Blanch noted with evident distaste, "houses where the passing traveller may refresh himself whilst he stands. He is not expected to stay long; neither is he permitted to sit down ... In some modern houses, with a vast amount of bar ornamentation and outside decoration, there is not so much as an empty barrel against which the weary traveller may lean."

The structure of the licensed liquor trade changed markedly in the course of the nineteenth century and Camberwell's experience offers a microcosm of the way in which this mirrored changes in the local demography and social structure. In 1787 Camberwell parish, still largely rural, had thirty-three public

houses, many doubtless deriving much business from day-trippers and passing travellers. Half a century later the number of pubs had quadrupled to 138 and there were also 96 'beershops', catering primarily for the poorer residents now living in the northern part of the parish. By the 1870s the disparities between rich and poor were even more clearly reflected in the institutions which supplied them with 'refreshment'. The number of pubs had actually fallen marginally, to 134, but the number of beershops had almost doubled to 172 and, to cater for the dining classes, there were also two licensed 'wine-houses' and 74 individuals – 'grocers and Italian warehousemen' – "licensed for the sale of various intoxicating liquors not to be consumed upon the premises."

Camberwell's greatest surge of population, between 1871 and 1901, saw the number of pubs more than double to 307, although a third of these were only licensed to sell beer or wine. There were, in addition, 134 off licences. It was, therefore, perhaps appropriate that in 1918 local licensed victuallers should take upon themselves the responsibility and expense of providing the Borough of Camberwell with the handsome mace which symbolised its authority.

104. A Band of Hope temperance mission photographed outside their hall in Oakley Place.

105. *One of the many local pubs ranged against the temperance missionaries – The Grove Hotel, Lordship Lane.*

PLEASURES FOR SALE

As working-hours shortened and real incomes rose commercial entertainment expanded to meet the needs of a new market no longer satisfied by annual fairs or the simpler pastimes offered by tavern proprietors. Music halls originated as 'free and easies', large rooms at the side or back of a pub, gas-lit, furnished with tables and chairs and with a small stage at one end for performers. One of the earliest was Lovejoy's, later the People's Palace of Varieties, at the old-established Rosemary Branch in Southampton Way. The Father Redcap at Camberwell Green, rebuilt in 1853, was another. From 1875 to 1879 Godfrey's Castle Musical Hall, otherwise the Bijou Palace of Varieties, flourished at 188 Camberwell Road. Anything but bijou were the two rival establishments built on opposite sides of Denmark Hill. The Metropole, later renamed the Empire, stood at the corner of Coldharbour Lane. Opened in 1894 it was intended to be, not a music hall, but a straight theatre, complete with private boxes, which would save the respectable bourgeoisie of the surrounding area from the inconvenience of traipsing up to the West End to see a good play. The Oriental Palace of Varieties, built in 1896, had the famous comedian Dan Leno as its chief backer. In 1899 it was relaunched as the Camberwell Palace of Varieties, with seating for two thousand. In complete contrast to the Metropole, the Palace was clearly aiming at the lower end of the market, pricing admission to boxes and the stalls at twopence per person, all other parts a penny. In addition to these attractions there were the Windsor Castle Music Hall in Cooper's Road and the Crown Theatre in Peckham – not to mention the gourmet delights of the eating-houses of Carlo Polti and Gussyppe Zaizaratti or the more spartan temptations of the coffee-rooms run by Joseph Hungerford and Mrs. Matilda Pengelly.

THE SILVER SCREEN

The first public, commercial demonstration of the movie camera was made in Paris in 1895. The public appetite for 'moving pictures' proved to be immense and by 1914 there were over 3,500 places in Britain where they could be seen. They were concentrated especially in urban areas with large, young, working-class populations. At first pictures were shown in music halls, the back rooms of pubs and even warehouses. In 1910 Peckham's venerable Hanover Chapel was converted to become a 'picture palace'. A number of well-publicised fires and crowd disasters soon led to stricter official regulation of premises and the construction of purpose-built venues. The New Grand Hall Cinematograph Theatre, opened in Camberwell New Road in 1912, could seat 840. Denmark Hill had the landmark Golden Domes (later

106. *The oriental opulence of the Camberwell Palace of Varieties, 1896.*

107. *The Camberwell Empire, c.1904, (opened in 1904 as the Metropole).*

108. *The Tower Cinema in Rye Lane, Peckham*

Rex, later Essoldo) and the Bijou (locally *a.k.a.* 'Bye Joe'). In 1914 Peckham High Street alone offered a choice of going to the Queen's Picture Theatre, the Peckham Picture Playhouse, the Central Hall Picture Palace, the Gem Picture Play House or the Hippodrome Picture Palace (formerly the Crown Theatre) – and there were another five cinemas round the corner in Rye Lane. In that same year film star Gladys Cooper came to open the Tower Cinema in person.

Eventually both the Empire and the Palace abandoned live entertainment in favour of films. The Empire, rebuilt as an Odeon in 1939, with seating for 2,470, closed in 1975 and was demolished in 1994. The Foyer Centre now occupies its site. By then all of Camberwell's other cinemas had also gone, although the Regal (closed 1961) had metamorphosed into a bingo hall and the Grand (closed 1968) into a snooker hall.

The final abolition of duties on newspapers in 1855 encouraged a flurry of optimistic speculations which launched such short-lived titles as the *South London News* and *South London Journal* and the more successful *South London Chronicle*, which survived, with interruptions, from 1859 to 1907. The *Camberwell and Peckham Times* (a.k.a. *South London Observer*) had a similarly chequered career between 1895 and 1969. In the interim the *South London Gazette*, *South London Mail*, *Dulwich Post and Herne Hill News* and *Dulwich*

109. *The selected design for Camberwell Green Public Baths. The architects were Spalding and Cross.*

110. *Camberwell Baths as actually built.*

111. *Dulwich Library.*

Echo had all come and gone. The palm for longevity has gone to the *South London Press*. Founded in 1865 by James Henderson, a radical Scot, it published its 10,000th edition in 1991.

THE NEW BOROUGH

Camberwell Council, on its own admission, "never hesitated to adopt a spirited municipal policy" and the years between the achievement of Borough status in 1900 and the outbreak of the Great War were marked by a sustained programme of expansion in public services and facilities. In 1900 an extensive municipal depot was laid out at Grove Vale, incorporating stabling for 88 horses. North Camberwell Public Library opened in 1902 and the adjoining Baths and Washhouses (cost £70,000) opened in 1905. That same year witnessed the completion of the Grove Vale Estate, one of the first in Britain to be built under powers granted by new enabling legislation. Begun in 1903, it consisted of 166 separate tenements in 89 properties, built at a cost of £46,902. Although far from cheap to rent at ten shillings a week they proved immediately popular with "the more respectable and thrifty members of the class for which they were intended – the struggling clerk, shopman etc.".

In 1907, after a three year campaign to prevent the

112. *Houses on the Grove Vale estate. Note the arms of the new Borough of Camberwell above the upper windows.*

113. *The 1934 remodelling of Camberwell's Town Hall incorporated the 1874 incarnation, still clearly visible at the left rear.*

area being built over, the Council opened Ruskin Park to the public. When Edward VII made an official visit to Camberwell on 20 July 1909 to lay the foundation stone of King's College Hospital at Denmark Hill, the Borough put itself *en fête*, decorating the streets profusely confident that its record already justified the reassuring municipal motto emblazoned on its banners and bunting – 'All's Well'.

114. *Edward VII doffs his top hat to a waiting camera during his 1909 visit to lay the foundation stone of King's College Hospital. The king was acutely aware of the role journalists and photographers could play in promoting a positive image of the monarchy.*

115. *Local politics in 1907. The scene outside the Municipal Reform Party headquarters in the Old Kent Road during the elections for the London County Council.*

At Prayer

PREACHERS AND CHURCHES

Moralist, educator, fund-raiser, reformer, comforter, dissident and resident intellectual – over the centuries the shifting currents of communal life have required local clergy to play a variety of roles, in the parish of Camberwell, no less than elsewhere.

The civil wars of the 1640s, and the religious turbulence which accompanied them, divided communities and even families. London was solidly for Parliament and a hotbed of religious fervour. Dulwich College nevertheless stood for the Royalists and as a result suffered the indignity of temporary administration by Parliament, destruction of its organ and many chapel furnishings and occupation by Cromwellian cavalry.

In the Reverend John Maynard (1600-1665), however, the parish possessed a self-declared Puritan who preached before the Long Parliament on no less than three occasions. Appointed Vicar of Camberwell in 1646, he resigned in 1651 to live in the lane leading "to the Old Kent Street road." Initially preaching in his own home, he was by 1657 able to sermonise in purpose-built premises in what is now appropriately called Meeting House Lane, Peckham.

In 1716 the Peckham Meeting House came into the charge of the energetic young Dr Samuel Chandler (1693-1766), who closed it down the following year to move the congregation to a larger building at the corner of what is now Rye Lane. Under his successor, Dr John Milner (1688-1757), who also doubled as a local headmaster and author of textbooks (see p.42), this building had to be enlarged yet further to accommodate a still growing congregation. The long (1801-1852!) ministry of Dr William Bengo Collyer marked a peak in the popularity of this place of worship. Within six years of his arrival two new side galleries had to be added for the flourishing flock he attracted to his services. In 1817 an entirely new church was built by a congregation which occasionally included even such social eminences as the Dukes of Kent and Sussex. These royal connections meant that what had once been known plainly as the Meeting House was henceforth referred to by a more elevated title – the Hanover Chapel.

The reconstruction of the Chapel took place against a background of vigorous church building elsewhere to meet the needs of the swelling suburb. In 1797 Camden Church in Peckham Road had been opened for a congregation of the Countess of Huntingdon's Connexion. In 1829 it became an Anglican chapel at ease and, following the distinguished ministry of Henry Melvill, a full parish church in 1844.

In Hill Street a proprietary chapel was built

116. *Rye Lane chapel – the 1863 incarnation.*

117. *Poster for a concert of Sacred Music at Hanover Chapel in 1824. This was a benefit event for one of the evening's performers J.H. Baildon "a Blind Lad, who has for some time been under the Patronage of the Congregation (while receiving gratuitous instruction on the Organ).*

Sacred Music

BY PERMISSION OF THE TRUSTEES OF

Hanover Chapel, Peckham,

A SELECTION

OF

SACRED MUSIC,

FROM

HANDEL, HAYDN, DR. BOYCE, &c.

WILL BE PERFORMED ON

THURSDAY, JUNE 3rd, 1821.

Principal Performers,

Miss GOODALL,

Miss TATTETT,

Mr. WALLIS, Mr. HARVARD, Mr. FRANKLIN,

Messrs. HAWKINS, and

MR. ATKINS.

The *CHORUS* will be complete in each Department.

THE WHOLE UNDER THE DIRECTION OF

Mr. J. H. BEE,

118. Camden Church in 1873.

in 1813-14; in 1865 it received an unusual new dedication to St John Chrysostom (Archbishop of Constantinople from 347 to 407). In 1952 Professor Pevsner observed that "the church has much atmosphere and should not be pulled down." It was pulled down in 1963.

Grove Chapel, Camberwell Grove was erected in 1819 and is now the oldest place of worship in Camberwell still meeting in its original building. It was not unusual for wealthy clergy to contribute to the furnishing of their churches by paying out of their own pocket for stained-glass windows or plate for communion but Joseph Irons, founder and first minister of Grove Chapel made a much more original and personal contribution. Trained as a carpenter, he fashioned its pulpit.

St George's, Wells Way was built in 1822-24 with funds from the Church Building Commissioners, set up by Parliament to provide new places of worship for areas where the population was increasing rapidly. Designed by Francis Bedford, a sometime resident of Camberwell Grove, its austere Doric 'Greek Revival' style was highly fashionable in that decade,

119. The handsome Rev. Henry Melvill (1798-1871) was the popular incumbent at Camden Chapel from 1829 to 1843.

120. Grove Chapel – Camberwell's oldest house of worship continuously occupied.

and conferred immediate cachet on a neighbourhood which, as Professor Pevsner caustically observed in 1952, "must have been handsome when the church was built". In 1825 the congregation of Denmark Place Baptist Church, founded in 1802, moved into a new home in Coldharbour Lane. In 1826 a new Friends Meeting House opened in Highshore Street, Peckham. Emmanuel Church, Camberwell Road was built in 1841-42 and may well have been the church in Dickens' *Great Expectations* in which Mr Wemmick impulsively marries Miss Skiffins, having parked his fishing-rod in the porch.

The reconstruction of the parish church of St Giles was occasioned, not by the need to respond to the pressures of population or to a tide of evangelical emotion but by a catastrophic conflagration which gutted the old church in 1841. Its successor was one of the earlier works of Sir George Gilbert Scott (1811-1878), who would go on to design the Midland Grand Hotel at St Pancras and the Albert Memorial and build up the largest architectural practice in the country. The artist and connoisseur Sir Charles Eastlake, first Director of the National Gallery and author of *Gothic Revival*, observed that "in the neighbourhood of London no church was considered in purer style." Fragments from the medieval church – a fourteenth-century sedilia and piscina and a number of Tudor monuments – were incorporated into the new fabric. The vicar, the Revd George Storie, contributed thirteenth-century stained-glass from

Trier in Germany, which became part of the west window. But the east window, a special glory, was designed by John Ruskin and his friend Edmund Oldfield and is the only surviving example of stained-glass by Ruskin. The organ was designed by the parish organist, Samuel Sebastian Wesley, grandson of the founder of Methodism, whose shrewish wife, Mary, lies buried somewhere in the churchyard. The organ was built by J.C. Bishop, founder of the firm of organ builders which was to bear his name. Almost as majestic as the rebuilt St Giles' were the 1844 church of St Paul's, Herne Hill and the 1848 church of St Matthew in Denmark Hill, designed by A.D. Gough, a prolific architect of suburban churches. Rebuilt in 1858 by G. G. Scott's pupil, G. E. Street, later President of the Royal Institute of British Architects, St Paul's was much praised by Ruskin.

PARISHES AND PARISHIONERS

Between the creation of the parish of St John the Evangelist, East Dulwich, in 1865 and that of St Barnabas, Dulwich in 1894, no less than fifteen more new Anglican parishes were created within the boundaries of what had anciently been the single parish of Camberwell. Speculative builders recognised that a decent church was essential if a new development was to attract the right sort of clientele and therefore often contributed to the building fund or even donated the site. At St Silas, Ivydale Road,

121. *St George's, Camberwell as depicted by the artist Schnebbelie soon after its opening. Note its proximity to the Grand Surrey Canal and the windmill in the background.*

a wall plaque recognised the benefactions of Edward Yates, who built three sizable estates in Camberwell. The laying of foundation stones was frequently an occasion for beneficial publicity, particularly if a celebrity could be secured to grace the day. At North Peckham Baptist Church the ceremony was performed by the most charismatic preacher of the times, Charles Haddon Spurgeon, and at Peckham Park Road Baptist Church the presiding luminary was the eminent railway contractor Sir Morton Peto.

Other notable places of worship dating from this period included the parish's first Roman Catholic church (1860), the handsome church of St John the Evangelist, Goose Green (1863-65), grandiose Methodist churches at Queen's Road (1864-65) ("really monstrously ugly" – Pevsner) and Barry Road (1873-74), a building in Camberwell New Road for the self-styled Catholic Apostolic Church (1876) (since 1963, St Mary's

Greek Orthodox Cathedral), the South London Baptist Tabernacle (1880) and the Calvary Temple at Councillor Street (1891) also for Baptists.

By 1902 resident worshippers in the newly established borough of Camberwell could choose between more than 150 churches, chapels and mission halls, more than five times as many as at mid-century. But, despite the proliferation of spiritual provision, attendance at worship continued to decline, as it did throughout the nation as a whole, to a local average of 25%. The researchers organised by social investigator Charles Booth commented that among male working men this amounted to "indifference only"; they were "not atheistical, but against church-going" and "quite willing to send their children to Sunday school and their wives to mothers' groups."

Within Camberwell, as nationally, average figures concealed significant local variations. Attendance was highest in Dulwich, where it involved one third

122. *(Top left) The rebuilt St Giles, Camberwell.*

123. *(Below) The Congregational Church, East Dulwich Grove.*

124. *(Top right) The first St Barnabas church – a temporary iron structure of 1891.*

125. St John the Evangelist, Goose Green, c.1904.

126. Peckham Rye Tabernacle Male Voice Choir, 1914.

of local residents and was almost entirely an Anglican phenomenon. In Peckham the figure was just a shade under the 25% average; but here only a third went to the Church of England as opposed to Nonconformist places of worship, the Baptists being almost as numerically strong as the Anglicans. In Camberwell, where attendance was under 19%, Anglicans accounted for less than a quarter of local worshippers and the strongest presence was represented by Congregationalists.

The organisation of worship was, of course, only one of the many functions which churches and chapels continued to perform. Even though their educational work was largely being taken over by state-sponsored schools, they continued to provide charitable relief for the poor and to serve as a focus of social activity through fêtes, bazaars, picnics, debates, improving lectures and classes and the support of choral societies and sports teams.

SETTLEMENTS
Orthodox ecclesiastical organisation was supplemented in south London by the 'settlement' movement which had begun in the East End in 1884 with the foundation of Toynbee Hall. There, idealistic young Oxford graduates committed themselves to living in what they saw as a socially and culturally deprived area, aiming to energise local community efforts towards self-improvement. Cambridge colleges similarly targeted the rapidly expanding working-class suburbs south of the Thames. In 1887 Corpus Christi College began its work in Peckham with a public meeting for worship under a railway arch in Wagner Street. In 1889 Trinity College established a centre, Trinity Court, in two Georgian houses in Camberwell Road. A few years later this merged with a new initiative to become Cambridge House. Avoiding directly religious activities, such as worship or Bible-study, Cambridge House volunteers set themselves "to provide, promote, assist and encourage work for the advancement of education or of religion, the relief of poverty, and other charitable and social work beneficial to the community, including the improvement of health by means of recreation or otherwise." Future Prime Minister, A.J. Balfour attended the inaugural meeting of Cambridge House and in 1898 the London historian Sir Walter Besant hailed it as "a centre of civilisation." One of the first priorities was the establishment of Hollington Boys Club, Comber Grove; another was the founding of a Children's Country Holiday Fund which by 1908 was sending almost 2,000 children away for a rural break each year. Other activities included the administration of an Infant Welfare Centre, supplying school meals to undernourished

127. Cambridge House Settlement in Camberwell Road.

children and operating a job-seekers' register and a 'Poor Man's Lawyer' service, offering free legal advice. These university enterprises were matched in the Nunhead area from 1890 onwards by a mission supported by a public school, Cheltenham College.

BEYOND THE PULPIT

The power to communicate is central to the effective propagation of the gospel. Declining religious belief and the availability of new mass media sharpened the challenge for the clergy in the twentieth century. The Rev. G.E. Thorn (1862-1943) transcended his Victorian roots to confront it. Appointed Congregational Minister to Clifton Church, Peckham in 1900, he relocated in 1908 to Peckham High Street at a site now occupied by a nightspot whose current patronage ironically echoes the name he gave to his foundation – Church of the Strangers. Eager to attract the indifferent by whatever means, he conducted services in the Crown Theatre and once preached dressed up as a biblical shepherd and on another occasion kitted himself out as a crusader to illustrate his chosen text – "Put on the whole armour of God."

Thorn's contemporary, Dr James Ebenezer Boon (1867-1941), a physician and President of the Peckham Christian Union, outdid him in July 1922 by becoming the first person in Britain to have a sermon broadcast by radio. Speaking from the Burdette Aerial Works at Blackheath, Boon was heard by 'listeners-in' at Christ Church, McDermott Road, Peckham, where a clothes-prop had been rigged up to support an aerial on the roof and an amplifier had been temporarily installed in front of the pulpit.

Less colourful, perhaps, but better known, is the Rt Rev. David Shephard (1929-), former cricket captain of England, who, as Bishop of Woolwich (1969-1975), lived at 12 Asylum Road, Peckham. While there he wrote the influential *Built as a City*, which explored the implications of his inner-city experience for modern evangelism and pastoral action.

A BEACON UPON THE HILL

Passionate, dynamic, autocratic 'General' William Booth (1829-1912), a Methodist lay preacher at seventeen, used a brilliantly imaginative marketing strategy to spread his gospel of 'Blood and Fire' through the slums of England. Playing on the jingoistic instincts of an imperialist age, he clothed the embattled troops of his Salvation Army in military uniforms and supported them with military-style bands which drew crowds to their street services and drowned out hecklers. "Why should the Devil have all the best tunes?" he demanded – though even he had doubts when he first heard *Champagne Charlie*

128. The statue of William Booth outside the William Booth Memorial Training College.

transformed into *Bless His Name, He Sets me Free*.

A sponsor of improved housing, legal aid schemes and assisted emigration projects, Booth published his programme for social improvement in his best-selling *In Darkest England And The Way Out* (1890) and spread his message through the uncompromisingly titled *War Cry*. By 1900, 5,500,000 in forty-seven countries were attending 'Sally Anny' services. In 1904, at eighty-five, Booth enlisted the aid of the newfangled motor-car to enable him to make a nationwide tour of evangelism. When he died in 1912 his funeral brought London to a standstill as half a million mourners spontaneously lined the streets of the capital. He died with a dream unfulfilled – to found an International University of Humanity. The William Booth Training College at Champion Park, Denmark Hill perhaps represents a partial realisation of his vision, combining in its architecture the austerity of a barracks with Gothic detailing reminiscent of an ancient seat of learning. The building was designed by Sir Giles Gilbert Scott (1880-1960), grandson of the architect of Camberwell parish church. Like his Bankside Power Station and Cambridge University Library, it is a bold composition in brick, dominated by a soaring tower.

Epidemics and Interments

Until around 1780 London required an annual intake of some five thousand newcomers a year simply to maintain its population. From then onwards there was a surplus of births over deaths. Coupled with continuing in-migration this, according to the 1811 census, pushed the population of the metropolis past the million mark. As a result the overcrowding of burials in the traditional church graveyards of the city centre became a scandal and a hazard to public health. The situation was aggravated to the point of crisis by the impact of an entirely novel and ter-rifying visitation in 1831-1832 – cholera. In Camberwell alone the epidemic carried off no less than 107 inhabitants. Parliament responded by au-thorising the establishment of major new cemeteries in what were then fringe areas of the capital, such as Kensal Green (1833) and West Norwood (1837). The new facilities established at Highgate (1839) and Nunhead (1840) were both managed by the London Cemetery Company.

129. The entrance to Nunhead Cemetery, 1997.

130. The monument in Camberwell Old Cemetery to three Armenian exiles, who were assassinated in Peckham by a fellow-countryman.

Nunhead's 30-acre 'Cemetery of All Saints' was laid out by J.B. Bunning, later architect to the City of London. Its permanent residents include such local worthies as coaching king, Thomas Tilling (1825-1903) and Sir George Livesey (1834-1908), chairman of the South Metropolitan Gas Company. Famed far beyond the locality were the very con-trasting achievements of two of Nunhead's other occupants. James Ward (1800-1884) was barefist champion of England from 1825 to 1832 at the close of the Regency era. Sir Polydor de Keyser (1832-1898) was a Belgian immigrant who worked his way up from a common waiter to proprietor of a four hun-dred bedroom luxury riverside hotel at Blackfriars, where Unilever House now stands. In 1887 he became the first Roman Catholic since the Reformation to serve as Lord Mayor of London.

The capital's inexorable expansion more than doubled its population in the first half of the nine-teenth century. Coupled with a second cholera out-break in 1848-1849 – which this time accounted for 504 victims in Camberwell – the continuing growth of London's population prompted the passage of the 1852 Metropolitan Interment Act. This encouraged local authorities to complement the efforts of private companies by providing additional burial facilities for the public. In 1854, the year in which a third

131. *At Nunhead, the funeral of six Boy Scouts drowned at sea in 1912.*

132. *Camberwell gravediggers, c.1900.*

133. Memorial to Scottish Political Martyrs in Nunhead. Sentenced to transportation "for advocating with fearless energy the principles of parliamentary reform" in 1793, immediately after the outbreak of war with revolutionary France, the cause of the five Scotsmen was still sufficiently celebrated for a subscription to be raised in 1837 for a monument to their sacrifice. Finally unveiled in 1851 it was inscribed with a defiant quotation from the defence of their leader Joseph Gerald: "The experience of all ages should have taught our rulers that persecution can never efface principles. Individuals may perish but truth is eternal."

and in 1864 Camberwell at last began to be connected to the capital's state-of-the-art steam-powered main drainage system. Taken together, these developments may explain why the death-toll from Camberwell's last cholera visitation fell dramatically to just 46.

What is now Old Camberwell Cemetery, established in 1856 by Camberwell Vestry, offered mourners the choice of three chapels – Roman Catholic, Church of England and Nonconformist, the latter two being designed by George Gilbert Scott (1811-1878), who had already proved himself locally with his rebuilding of Camberwell's own parish church of St Giles. By the 1890s, Camberwell Cemetery, praised at its inception as 'eminently picturesque', was deemed to have fallen into a state of scandalous neglect, perhaps a fitting place in which to lose the memory of George Yanni who, in 1903, murdered three fellow Armenian exiles in their club in Peckham Rye.

Camberwell New Cemetery, opened in 1927, affords a last resting-place to both the spiritually and physically strenuous. Wilfrid Kitching, General of the Salvation Army from 1954 to 1963, "passed to glory" there. William Pullum (1887-1960), world weightlifting champion, rests there at last, as does popular Freddie Mills (1919-1965), world light heavyweight boxing champion from 1948 to 1950. The imposing chapel was designed by Sir Aston Webb, who had, before the war, designed the facades of the Victoria & Albert Museum and Buckingham Palace.

cholera epidemic carried off a peak number of victims in Camberwell – 553, a Camberwell Burial Board was finally established. The Metropolis Management Act of 1855 gave Camberwell Vestry more comprehensive powers over sewerage, drainage and cleansing

134. The chapel at Camberwell New Cemetery, designed by Sir Aston Webb.

135. *Before the establishment of Board Schools, Ragged Schools were provided, usually by missions, for the poorest of children. A Ragged School dinner in Camberwell is shown here.*

Healthy Mind, Healthy Body

NEW EDUCATIONAL PROVISION

The second half of the nineteenth century witnessed the parallel development of two important movements in British educational provision. One was the piecemeal emergence of a system of free mass elementary instruction, nationally supervised but locally administered. The other was a renascence of the elite public school system under the impact of the 'Rugby revolution' wrought by its charismatic headmaster, Dr Thomas Arnold, which imparted a new rigour to the curriculum and an exalted sense of vocation to those who were called upon both to deliver and to receive it.

In Camberwell the mass system was fostered by the London School Board which reckoned, when it

took up its work in the 1870s, that existing, mostly church-based, schools in Camberwell, Peckham and Dulwich, offered some seven thousand free places – less than a third of the number needed. A vigorous building programme dotted the landscape with solidly-built, multi-storey Board Schools over succeeding decades.

Previous patterns of provision, of course, overlapped with these changes. Camberwell's local tradition of house-based, small-scale instruction for the offspring of gentlefolk was only gradually eroded. This included, for example, the rival ladies' schools run in 1868 by Mrs Susan White and Miss Mary Clarke within doors of each other, just off Peckham Rye, while nearby in Nunhead Lane was a similar establishment under the governance of the Misses Louisa and Emily Grove, who were themselves only yards from James Procter Hawkins' "preparatory school for young gentlemen". And there were at least three more similar institutions within minutes' walking distance in the surrounding streets. But

136. A typical Board School in Adys Road, East Dulwich

137. The entwined London School Board motif on the side of Ivydale Road School.

these were essentially relics of the past. They were hard pushed by the creation of Board schools, and those with much grander names and not on the face of it trawling for the same pupils as the Board schools, were doomed by the renascence of Dulwich College. In that same period two up-market schools went out of business: Camberwell Collegiate School (demolished 1867) and Denmark Hill Grammar School (closed 1873).

RENASCENCE AT DULWICH COLLEGE

A considerable change had occurred at Dulwich College. As D. H. Allport has observed, with as much candour as elegance, "the history of the College for some 238 years was little more than the leisurely administration of a great estate. The education of Dulwich boys and the care of twelve poor almsfolk sat lightly on the 'Gentlemen of the College'." In an age rife with reform the old insouciance could not hope to escape searching scrutiny. The result was the Dulwich College Act of 1857, breaking Alleyn's original foundation into separate parts, which, after further statutory adjustments in 1882, led the estate as such to be administered by one set of Governors, the picture gallery and boys' schools by another and James Allen's Girls' School by a third.

Dulwich College found its own Dr Arnold in the Revd A. J. Carver, an outstanding scholar of classics,

138. Tuition at Dulwich College, 1828, before its reformation. From an oil painting by W.C. Horsley.

139. Alfred J. Carver, headmaster of Dulwich College.

mathematics and theology. A Trinity man himself, he recruited three more Trinity men to his staff, plus seven other Cambridge graduates and five Oxonians. The teacher of physics he appointed held a doctorate, as did two of the four Masters of Modern Languages. Even the School Secretary had an M.A. And there were additional specialists to teach chemistry, geology and singing, as well as a Drill Master and four instructors in drawing.

The rebirth of the College was both nurtured and symbolised by its translation into imposing new buildings in an Italianate style. Designed by Charles Barry the Younger, son of the famed architect of the House of Commons, they were opened in 1870 by no less a person than the Prince of Wales. Their splendour was purchased at the cost of some £80,000, derived from sales of land to railway companies. Under the guidance of Carver, and his no less estimable successor, Gilkes, the school grew rapidly in reputation and steadily in numbers, from 300 in 1870 to 680 by 1896 and 900 by 1918.

By then Alleyn's School, which had grown out of the Lower Department of the refounded College, had firmly established its own identity, having moved into new buildings of its own in 1887. In 1907 Alleyn's

140. *The old buildings at Dulwich College.*

became a pioneer among day schools by introducing the 'house system' as a focus for discipline and loyalty. James Allen's Girls' School likewise acquired new premises in East Dulwich Grove in 1886, at which time it had 122 pupils. Its pioneering contribution was to use its extensive grounds for the study of plants in their natural habitats, an early excursion into the now fashionable field of ecology.

REFOUNDATIONS

Wilson's Grammar School also entered a new era, a metamorphosis the more profound in that the continuity of its existence had been broken for almost four decades. In 1843 the Governors found themselves in dispute with a Camberwell parishioner over a matter which had nothing to do with education as such. They won their case, but, disastrously, were forced to bear costs so huge that they were obliged to close the school and sell off everything except the land it stood on. Thanks to the doughty efforts of successive Governors and the support of Camberwell residents the school was finally reconstituted in 1880 and moved into brand-new buildings in 1882.

Another re-foundation, Mary Datchelor School, took its name from the donor of a charitable bequest of 1726, whose funds were redirected to provide a sound education for middle-class girls. It moved into its Camberwell Grove premises in 1876.

141. *The Old Grammar School, designed in 1842 by Charles Barry Snr. It later housed the Lower School of the reformed Dulwich College, then from 1887 became the Village Reading Room, then a working men's club. Dulwich Hamlet F.C. was founded here at a meeting in 1893.*

142. *The new Dulwich College buildings – an approved official photograph, noteworthy for the total absence of boys.*

SPORT

Modern sport was effectively invented in nineteenth century England and dominated both popular culture and much of the leisure time of all classes, as well as providing new forms of employment. Camberwell amply illustrates its popularity, for it not only boasted a nationally important stadium for cycling, as well as a roller-skating rink but also a highly successful amateur football team in Dulwich Hamlet F.C., 'the Arsenal of amateur football'. Peckham even had two factories manufacturing 'athletic goods' and several more making bicycles. And Dulwich was virtually re-landscaped to accommodate the demand for specialised playing facilities. The 1870 Ordnance Survey map of Dulwich shows the entire area west of Gallery Road and its northerly continuation as open fields. The 1916 edition shows it sub-divided into the Alleyn Cricket Ground, the Tudor Athletic Ground, Christ Church Cricket Ground, Borough Polytechnic Athletic Ground, Lloyd's Register Cricket Ground, Farrow's Bank Sports Ground, London County Athletic Grounds, Westminster City School Playing Ground and the Alleyn Football Ground. A similar transformation occurred on the Common east of College Road, which, by 1916, had been largely carved up to accommodate Camberwell Grammar School Athletic Ground, the Alleynian R.F.C., a 'tennis ground' and Dulwich and Sydenham Hill Golf Course.

Two meadows converted into cricket fields were among the visitor attractions at the Greyhound inn in Dulwich. Goose Green was the location of Harry Hampton's Ground, which witnessed the cricketing debut of Nicholas Wanostrocht, (1804-1876), great nephew of local headmaster Dr Wanostrocht. He went on to appear at Lord's playing for a Camberwell XI against Uxbridge. Far more important than his playing career, however, was his influence, under the pen-name of 'N. Felix', on the development of the game as the author of *Felix on the Bat* (1845), the first authoritative account of the game's rules, conventions and techniques.

Dulwich Hamlet F.C. grew out of a team founded in 1893 by the Dulwich Hamlet School Old Boys' association and members of a gymnastics class organised at St Barnabas Church. Initially, they played on the ground used by the school in Woodwarde Road, bringing their own goal posts from storage in the garden of the Crown Inn and changing their kit at the Old Grammar School. Success brought a wider membership and a new ground in Sunray Avenue and then in 1912 a permanent home at Dog Kennel Hill. After the interruption of the war years Dulwich Hamlet F.C. became a dominant force in the amateur game, winning the Isthmian League in 1920, 1926, 1933 and 1949. (It was won in 1929 and 1930 by another local team, Nunhead.) In the 1920 FA Amateur Cup Final, held at Millwall, Dulwich beat Tufnell Park by the only goal of the match after extra time. In a fourth round replay in the FA Cup in 1922 Dulwich conceded seven goals to a single player, Billy Minter of St Albans – and still won 8-7! The FA Amateur Cup final held at Upton Park saw Dulwich thrash Marine of Liverpool 7-1. In 1934 and 1937 they repeated their triumph at the same ground, defeating Leyton on both occasions. Little wonder that in 1931 the club felt justified in opening stands which could accommodate 10,000 fans.

The cycling craze hit Britain in the 1890s, following the invention of the pneumatic tyre. South London, with its large population of increasingly prosperous clerks and tradesmen, who would buy a bicycle to get them to work and use it for excursions at weekends, constituted a ready recruiting-ground for cycling clubs. Soon there were rival clubs in different parts of the borough – the Dulwich Bicycle Club, the East Dulwich Cycling Club and the South Roads Club. In 1910 Edwardes cycle shop opened in the Camberwell Road, its proprietor a former all-England cycling champion. Even tiny Dulwich supported its own cycle-maker.

In 1892 a leading amateur racing cyclist, George Lacey-Hillier, founded the London County Athletic Ground Limited and built a stadium at Herne Hill which combined an outer cycle track of rolled ballast with an inner cinder track for athletics and, in the middle, a rugby pitch. This facility was destined to become a leading venue for competitive cycling and successive improvements were made to it, such as the installation of a banked concrete track in 1896. On Good Friday each year it hosted the Southern Counties Cycling Union Champion of Champions meeting. In 1926 J.E. Holdsworth set a world record for distance covered in 24 hours – 534 miles and 1,500 yards. In 1948 Herne Hill was the scene of the cycling events of the XIV Olympiad. Mario Ghella of Italy beat home favourite and World Sprint Champion Reg Harris to take gold in the 1,000 metres race.

In 1876 one of Britain's first purpose-built roller-skating rinks opened on the east side of Grove Lane, opposite Denmark Hill station. A layer of crushed lava, imported from the slopes of Mount Vesuvius to improve its surface, gained it the name of the Lava Rink. In 1885 'rink polo' – hockey on roller-skates – was played here – the first time in England.

The rink was destroyed by fire shortly after the First World War.

143. *'Nicholas Felix', the pen name of Nicholas Wanostrocht, the author of the first authoritative work on the rules of cricket.*

PARKS

Dulwich Park was once part of Dulwich Common. In 1885 the area was presented *gratis* to the public by the Governors of Dulwich College, thus preserving it ever since from the encroachments of speculative builders. Victorian designers added a tree-lined carriage-drive, an aviary and a three-acre boating lake before its ceremonial opening by the first chairman of the newly-established London County Council in June 1890. Lt. Col. Sexby, the L.C.C.'s first superintendent of parks, commented approvingly that "it is particularly free from the loafing population which lolls upon the grass in St James's Park thick as windfalls in an orchard. Though open to all, it is specially frequented by a superior class of visitors from the immediate neighbourhood." Sexby's assessment was later authoritatively confirmed by royal patronage, as George V's formidable consort, Queen Mary, proved a regular visitor, taking especial interest in the park's fine display of azaleas and rhododendrons.

Peckham Rye Common was likewise once common land, where medieval villagers could graze livestock and gather firewood. Locals assembled to defend it from encroachment in 1766 and 1789 and in 1864 to challenge the presence of the 32 vans carrying Wombwell's Wild Beast Show. Shortly afterwards a proposal was raised to build houses over the Common, the lord of the manor declaring a residual ancient right to grant permission for such development. Camberwell Vestry bought him off in 1868 and in 1882 sold the land on to the Metropolitan Board of Works, placing it in the public domain for good. Over the course of the following decade a local campaign raised funds to purchase the adjoining Homestall Farm, which was landscaped and opened on Whit Monday 1894 as Peckham Rye Park.

One Tree Hill, also known as Honor Oak Hill, rises some 345 feet above the Thames and was once surmounted by a signal station used by the East India Company and the Admiralty to communicate news of shipping movements in the Channel. The long vanished oak from which it took its name once served to mark a county and parish boundary separating Camberwell (Surrey) from Lewisham (Kent). In 1896 the local golf club decided to enclose the hill with a six foot high fence, thereby blocking five traditional public rights of way. On 10 October 1897 fifteen thousand protesters gathered and broke down sections of the fence. A week later they returned in numbers three times, some claimed six times, as strong – to find five hundred police waiting for them. A stand-off ensued until 1904 when Camberwell Council bought the land from its owner, opening it to the public in August 1905.

In 1904 the former grounds of Dane House came up for sale, apparently destined to become yet an-

144. Ruskin Park, c.1904.

other housing estate – until local resident Frank Trier, shrewdly capitalising on the recent death of the area's most prominent former inhabitant, conjured up a Ruskin Park Purchase Committee. Hoping to gain support from "admirers of the great man of letters", the Committee also gained the endorsement of such bodies as the Commons and Footpaths Preservation Society and the Metropolitan Public Gardens Association. With financial contributions forthcoming from the L.C.C., the borough councils of Camberwell, Southwark and Lambeth and numerous local residents, 24 acres were successfully purchased in 1906 and opened to the public in February 1907. Soon afterwards it was proposed to build houses on an adjoining block of land. Trier once again remobilised his forces and achieved the purchase of a twelve acre extension, opened to the public in February 1910. A bowling green now covers what was once a kitchen garden. The base of what was a terracotta sundial, adorned with Tudor rose designs, forlornly marks the site of the house where Mendelssohn composed his *Spring Song*.

The very name of Belair echoes the eighteenth-century's preoccupation with salubrious situations. *Belair* mansion, which featured a spectacular spiral staircase, remained a private home until 1938, its last occupant being Sir Evan Spicer, head of the famous papermaking firm of that name. During the war the house, commandeered to serve as an army transport headquarters, was badly knocked about by its temporary occupants. The Governors of Dulwich College, whose property it was, meanwhile looked in vain for a new squire and in 1945 finally granted the house and its grounds to the Council on a ninety-nine year lease. The estate was opened as a public park in 1947 but more pressing demands on the public purse left the expensive business of refurbishing the house in abeyance. By 1960 Belair House was so far decayed that the Council was eager to demolish it altogether but the College Governors pressed suc-

145.   *The public opening of One Tree Hill, 7 August 1905.*

cessfully for the enforcement of a restoration clause which had been inserted as a condition of the leasing agreement they had granted. To the Council's dismay it was subsequently revealed that the house had been built over a well, which had to be filled in, at much expense, as a prelude to large-scale rebuilding. Belair is now a community facility. Its surrounding park boasts over forty different species of trees, including such rarities as an aged cork oak and a white mulberry from China. The winding, serpentine lake is the only substantial stretch of the ancient River Effra remaining above ground.

Burgess Park represents an environmental revolution. The vast majority of London parks have been created by defending existing open lands against commercial demands for space for houses, roads, railways or business premises. But Burgess Park stands on what was once an entirely urbanised area. comprising some thirty streets and nine hundred homes, complete with their attendant schools, churches and factories and a goodly stretch of the Grand Surrey Canal. Writing in 1983 Hunter Davies recorded with unconcealed astonishment that "No one, anywhere in the world, has ever bulldozed the urban landscape on such a scale before, just to produce a bit of open space." (*A Walk Round London Parks*). Burgess Park was produced by an involuntary partnership between the Luftwaffe and the London County Council. Wartime bombing created

a semi-wilderness which, in 1943, far-sighted planners re-interpreted as an opportunity to establish an open space in an area two miles or more from any other one. From the outset – most unusually – they were prepared to contemplate a time-scale of half a century to realise their project, acquiring individual properties piecemeal to complete a jig-saw puzzle which was ultimately envisioned as covering 135 acres. The core component, inelegantly and bureaucratically christened North Camberwell Open Space, was opened in 1950. By 1965 it had expanded to fifteen acres, by 1974 to more than forty. In 1982 an eight-acre lake for boating and fishing was opened. It was the first recreational lake to be constructed in inner London this century and the first ever to be created on formerly built-up land. By 1983 eighty-eight acres, an area the size of St James's Park, was in use.

In 1995 Multi-cultural Gardens, with Oriental, Mediterranean, African and Caribbean, Islamic and English sections, were opened. At the western end of the park, an ironic echo of the past, stands one of the few survivals from the site's past – the last 'Parker' kiln left in London. Dating from the early nineteenth century, it was erected to produce the lime which was an essential component of the 'Roman cement' which once bound together the now vanished buildings whose foundations sleep beneath the grass.

The Ordeals of War

LOCAL HEROES

During the first two years of the First World War over 100,000 volunteers joined up at Camberwell Town Hall, which was the chief recruiting station for South London. Of these, 4,500 went into the 33rd (Camberwell) Divisional Artillery, commanded by Major Fred Hall, the MP for Dulwich.

The main local unit, however, was the First Surrey Rifles, which traced its origin to the Volunteer regiment founded in 1859 at the time of a war scare with France. Within four days of war being declared in August 1914, a first battalion was up to full strength and a second being raised. As the 21st London Regiment the first battalion served at the battles of Mons, Ypres and Loos and distinguished itself, at great cost of lives, taking a line of German forts at High Wood during the later stages of the Somme offensive. Of the 550 men and nineteen officers who went into the attack on 15 September 1916 only sixty

men and two officers returned to camp the morning after the action. The name of High Wood Barracks, built in Lordship Lane in 1938, commemorates this action. The second battalion of the regiment served farther afield, initially at Arras but then in Greece, finally taking part in Allenby's Palestine campaign, capturing Jericho and Jerusalem.

Three Camberwell men won the Victoria Cross in the course of the conflict.

On 1 November 1914, at the first battle of Ypres, Drummer John Bent, when all his officers had been killed, assumed command of his comrades and held his trench against the continuing German offensive. Able Seaman Albert McKenzie, serving in the Royal Navy with *H.M.S. Vindictive*, won his V.C. for his part in storming the mole at the German submarine base at Zeebrugge in April 1918. Ironically, having survived that risky enterprise, he was to die of influenza later that same year and is buried in Camberwell Old Cemetery. Wing-Commander F.A. Brock, of the firework manufacturing family, who devised the smoke-screen which was an important element in Zeebrugge raid, was

146. For King and Country – a leaflet advertising a procession and band concert in aid of recruitment, May 1915. The 33rd Division of the Royal Field Artillery was a Camberwell unit. Note the minimum physical requirements – height 5' 1", chest 33".

147. Over There: an inscription added to a local family
monument recalls a son buried in Flanders.

killed leading a storming-party at that same action.
Lance Corporal Arthur Cross of the First Surrey
Rifles was decorated for single-handedly capturing
two machine guns during the final German offensive
of June 1918. In addition to these Camberwell residents five Old Alleynians also won VCs during the
Great War.

HEALING HANDS

To treat the large numbers of wounded shipped back
across the Channel from France and Flanders much
of southern England was turned into a vast medical
reception area. King's College Hospital, which had
only completed its move into its Camberwell premises
in 1913, became for the most part, the Fourth London
General Military Hospital. The newly-established
Maudsley Hospital specialised in the treatment of
'shell-shock' as the army grudgingly conceded, in the
face of overwhelming evidence, that men could be
disabled mentally as well as physically. Dulwich
Hospital became Southwark Military Hospital and
Kingswood House in Dulwich was turned over to
the Canadian forces to serve as a convalescent home.
The author Vera Brittain, a V.A.D. (Voluntary Aid
Detachment) nurse was billeted in a cheerless hostel
at 31 Champion Hill while serving in the military
hospital in Cormont Road, Lambeth which had
formerly been St Gabriel's Teachers' Training
College.

Another converted institution was the skating rink
on Grove Lane, which became a military depot.
Dulwich Hamlet F.C., its ranks depleted by the rush
of players to volunteer, ceased to function and its
changing rooms were used to store the harness of
the Camberwell Gun Brigade. Other visible signs of
the war effort included the drilling of recruits and
grazing of military horses on Goose Green, and the
unaccustomed sight of women heaving sacks of coke
into the cellars of suburban homes on behalf of the
South Metropolitan Gas Works. Rather less visible,
one imagines, was the work being carried out at

148. Women stokers tend the ovens of the South Metropolitan
Gas Works during the First World War.

149. Zeppelin raid damage during the First World War.

Brockwell House, Herne Hill where the staff of the Wellcome Physiological Laboratory were producing antitoxins to combat tetanus, serums to treat gas gangrene and vaccines to ward off outbreaks of typhoid in the trenches.

THE ENEMY ABOVE

The 'Great War for Civilization' brought a new dimension to conflict between nations – the aerial bombing of civilian populations. Non-combatant Londoners found themselves at least spasmodically in the front line. Camberwell's worst single incident occurred on the night of 19/20 October 1917, when flats at the corner of Albany Road and Calmington Road were demolished by an aerial torpedo dropped from a Zeppelin, killing twelve people, including two children. A memorial tablet was placed there after the war but has been removed – along with Calmington Road – as a result of the creation of Burgess Park. Ten other deaths occurred elsewhere in the borough as a result of enemy action.

THE ENEMY WITHIN

Despite the presence of a long-established and ultra-respectable German community in its midst, Camberwell proved just as prone to anti-German hysteria as the East End, where luckless Russian Jews had their windows smashed and their businesses wrecked on account of the foreign-sounding names of the proprietors. In Camberwell, it was not the haute bourgeoisie of Champion Hill who suffered; discreetly sheltered behind high walls and shrubbery, they were safe from the fury of the mob. The victims were, rather, the all too visible butchers, Melsheimer of Albany Road and Eifler of Camberwell Green, and bakers Sturmer and Frieburger of Camberwell Road and Moth of Wyndham Road. As if to expunge even the memory of the hated aliens, Leipsic Road, named for the city of Leipzig, was re-christened to become Comber Grove.

150. Camberwell Town Hall decorated to celebrate the end of the First World War.

151. *French colonial troops pass through Camberwell in a victory parade in 1918.*

152. *The memorial in Camberwell Old Cemetery to the 22 civilians killed locally by enemy action during the First World War.*

FOREBODINGS AND PREPARATIONS

In 1937 Camberwell Borough Council received instructions from government to recruit and train an Air Raid Precautions (A.R.P.) organisation and to select premises for their use in the event of war. At the time of the Munich crisis the following year the Council arranged for the distribution of gas masks, a step which unmistakably underlined the gravity of the situation.

By the summer of 1939 the failure of the Chamberlain government's appeasement strategy had become sufficiently clear to provoke active recruitment in the borough for the A.R.P. service, auxiliary firemen and female volunteers to assist with evacuation. Apparently undeterred by the worsening international situation, members of the British Union of Fascists continued to demonstrate outside Camberwell Town Hall. Dulwich also boasted, if that could be said to be the word, its own branch of the National Socialist League, a breakaway faction of the B.U.F., founded in 1937 and headed by local resident William Joyce, later to win broadcasting notoriety as Nazi stooge and propagandist 'Lord Haw-Haw'.

Partial evacuation exercises were organised by several schools on the eve of the summer holidays. In August 1939 there was a 'BIG BLACK OUT' rehearsal. The evacuation of children in earnest began in September. Alleyn's School senior section initially

153. *A Peckham Red Cross contingent practises working in gas masks before the outbreak of the Second World War.*

went to the Maidstone area but ended up eventually at Rossall in Lancashire, where staff gamely guarded the sea wall by night. Dulwich College Prep. followed a similarly nomadic course from Cranbrook in Kent to a hotel at Bettws-y-Coed in Wales. The pupils of James Allen's Girls' arrived in Hollingbourne, Kent rather to the consternation of locals who had been briefed to expect pregnant mothers from the East End of London; their eventual course took them full circle, via Sevenoaks, back to Dulwich. Dulwich College did likewise, following an unsatisfactory excursion to Tonbridge. The children of St. George's School, initially sent to Sevenoaks, were relocated in June 1940 to Bideford in Devon. In addition to the organised exportation of the borough's schoolchildren some two thousand homes were abandoned by their owners. Most would be requisitioned to provide shelter for over 5,000 local families rendered homeless by enemy action.

During the period of the 'Phoney war', preceding the German spring offensives of 1940, the Council perfected its Civil Defence arrangements, establishing 67 Wardens' posts throughout the borough, a Mobile First Aid Unit, a Gas Identification Service,

a De-contamination Service and a reserve Report and Control Centre at Grove Vale depot in case the Town Hall should be put out of action. Later in the war the Council would lay plans for the reception and accommodation of up to 27,000 refugees from the coastal areas of southern England in the event of an invasion.

In July 1940, as the country hourly anticipated invasion, the Mayor of Camberwell appealed for weapons on behalf of the newly-established Local Defence Volunteers, soon to be renamed the Home Guard. After a week he found himself in possession of a single pair of binoculars. The following month the Council and the A.R.P. service combined forces to raise a force of a hundred bicycling couriers and announced themselves ready even to consider 'girl applicants'. At North Dulwich females came into their own as W.A.A.F.s manned the barrage balloons and received the compliment of being 'adopted' by Camberwell Rotary Club. R.A.F. Balloon Command set up its local headquarters at The Platanes, Champion Hill. Piecemeal the borough acquired an increasingly martial air as Belair became the headquarters of Dulwich Home Guard and a depot for the

154. *Camberwell's decontamination service, established to combat the effects of (mistakenly) anticipated chemical warfare.*

Army Ordnance Corps and the Auxiliary Territorial Service; holes 8 to 14 at the golf club were commandeered for military use; and Gallery Road was cordoned off to serve as an Army lorry park. A rocket battery was stationed on the sports fields of Dulwich Common. Later in the war Italian prisoners of war would be accommodated in huts on Peckham Rye and German POWs in huts in Croxted Road, near its junction with Ildersley Grove.

THE INNER MAN

During the First World War rationing had been implemented belatedly, haphazardly and unfairly. Two decades later the significance of 'the kitchen front' was appreciated from the outset by government and population alike.

In August 1939 households were advised to lay in a week's supply of food for emergencies. Ration books were distributed in September, and November was announced as the deadline for registering with the retailers of one's choice. Rationing began in

earnest in January 1940 with a weekly allowance per person of half a pound of sugar and four ounces of bacon or ham. The latter restriction encouraged the formation of Pig Clubs, especially where communal feeding arrangements provided a ready supply of peelings, scraps and left-overs. Dulwich College had one and so did a number of local A.R.P. posts and anti-aircraft batteries. The 'Dig for Victory' campaign met an equally enthusiastic response. The Borough made land available in its parks at an annual rental of five shillings (25p) per allotment. By August 1940 the Dulwich Allotment Society could boast some three hundred members, and in December 1940 its two most prolific producers were announced to have grown almost a ton of vegetables between them. A generally dull dietary landscape was enlivened periodically by unaccustomed incidents. In October 1941 local children under six were allocated a one pound entitlement of oranges.

In October 1942 a 'British Restaurant' opened to the inhabitants of Dulwich in the Grafton Hall, Village Way. Despite its morale-boosting name (an in-

155. *A Civil Defence exercise - extricating a 'casualty' from bomb wreckage. Note the metal stretcher, subsequently widely recycled as fencing on public housing schemes.*

spired Churchillian coinage) to its potential clientele it still evidently bore all the connotations of its original designation – Communal Feeding Centre. Such fastidious reluctance moved the local representative of the Londoners' Meal Service to express her regret that Dulwich residents should feel that patronising such establishments was "not the thing to do." Perhaps some compensation for their reluctance to participate in communal messing was derived from the posters devised by Dulwich artist James Fitton in 1943 for the Ministry Food, urging Britons that it *was* very much the thing to do.

BLITZED!

For Camberwell the aerial war began in August 1940 when the first bombs dropped on the borough. Ironically the first bomb to fall in the Dulwich area destroyed William Joyce's former home in Allison Grove. In September a raid condemned the audience at the Odeon, Peckham to a seven hour stint of confinement, relieved by usherette-led bouts of com-

munity singing. During the same month a high explosive bomb made a direct hit on a street shelter in Albrighton Road, Dog Kennel Hill, killing thirty-seven and injuring another thirteen. The incident was judged by the relevant authorities sufficiently significant to merit a consolatory visit by the King and Queen. Another incident in the same month killed nine members of the Wright family of Medlar Street in a public shelter on Camberwell Green. The massive raid of 29 December 1940, which set a ring of fire around St Paul's Cathedral, also inflicted numerous casualties on the passengers and crews of trams which had stopped outside Camberwell Town Hall.

By February 1941 the Borough Council had made two mobile kiosks available to be sent to bombed areas to save victims from trekking round different departments to arrange for new ration books, temporary accommodation etc. In March of that year the garages of luxury flats on Champion Hill were requisitioned to serve as a mortuary. In January 1943 a Luftwaffe raid mounted in reprisal for the bombing of Berlin devastated Lytcott Grove with a parachute mine, killing ten.

The 'second blitz' began in May 1944 when the first of 81 V-1 'doodlebugs' fell within the borough boundaries. In July Dulwich College was hit and at the end of the same month another raid severely damaged Dulwich Picture Gallery, destroying the mausoleum where its benefactors were interred. The most valuable paintings in the collection had long since been removed to the safety of a Welsh mine but a hundred remaining items were mutilated to varying degrees. On an August Saturday afternoon 23 shoppers were killed and another forty-two seriously hurt in the crowded Co-op in Lordship Lane. It took two days and nights to recover all the casualties from the wreckage. By October 36 V-1 incidents were reported in the Dulwich area alone. In part this represents a triumph for the misinformation disseminated by British counter-intelligence which misled the enemy into believing that the flying-bombs were overshooting the capital to fall harmlessly in open country to the north. Redirected in response to these reports the V-1s

became concentrated on the south-east of London, sparing the densely-populated centre at the expense of the leafy suburbs. By September over a third of the borough's homes were roofless. In October Camberwell was listed as the fourth most heavily damaged area in the entire metropolis. With only a hundred and fifty men available at that time to undertake repairs it was impossible to keep pace with the damage and the borough acquired the dubious distinction of being the only one in London to fail to meet its repair target that winter. In the event large-scale importation of men from other parts of the country was required to make good the shortfall of labour. Repair work went on until 1948, by which time the bill had passed £10,000,000. This programme required the creation of the largest single service undertaken by the borough council in the first half century of its existence, employing some 2,000 men.

The first of eight V-2 attacks began in November 1944. A single rocket falling in Friern Road and Etherow Street killed 24 people. The last V-1 fell in Court Lane in January 1945, killing seven, injuring

156. ARP workers searching the debris of wrecked houses in Camberwell. In the foreground survivors scavenge usable belongings.

36. In March the Council announced the damage inflicted on the borough's housing stock over the course of the conflict. Of some 40,000 dwellings only 10% escaped damage altogether. 9,062 were seriously damaged and 5,650 destroyed outright.

SECRET WAR

From 1942 to 1944 the handsome colonnaded residence on Dulwich Common known as Glenlea became *Huize Anna* (House of Anna), a residence and training base for Dutch agents. Of the 34 agents who passed through there the first and last were both killed while flying to their assignments. Nineteen others were arrested, of whom five survived. Thirteen evaded capture to complete their missions successfully. Huize Anna graduate Bram Grisnigt was liberated by the Russians from Ravensbruck concentration camp and returned to marry a former pupil of James Allen's Girls' School in Emmanuel Church, West Dulwich.

KEEP SMILING THROUGH

High morale was regarded by government as being significant in encouraging civilians to endure privation, just as it was in sustaining servicemen's willingness to fight. After an initial period of closure at the behest of the government, the borough's cinemas reopened to provide escapism throughout the rest of the war. A visit to the 'movies' gave the chance to appreciate the talents of former local residents Ray Milland and Roddy McDowell, child star of the 1941 Welsh weepie *How Green Was My Valley*. Another local talent was Pat Sibley, born in Dulwich and a former pupil of Sacré Coeur Convent in Honor Oak, who was to find fame as a singer with the Ambrose Orchestra under the name Anne Shelton. In July 1941 the L.C.C. was sponsoring Sunday afternoon band concerts in parks, while the A.R.P. was organising a swimming gala, the final of its inter-post darts competition and a dance which attracted 250 guests and the Mayor and Mayoress. A year later the L.C.C. supported the government's 'Stay at Home' holiday campaign by organising a cricket match in Dulwich Park between Camberwell Civil Defence and the Dulwich police, followed by a concert in the

evening. Between 1943 and 1944 membership of the Dulwich and Sydenham golf club actually rose by 10%. Dulwich College Music Club kept up the cultural tone of the neighbourhood by presenting chamber music concerts on Sunday afternoons. A number of public libraries were, however, closed down as a result of enemy action and the Old Kent Road Baths completely demolished.

Vandalism of public air raid shelters proved to be a continuing nuisance and on one occasion men of the Dulwich Heavy Rescue Service defied the official ban on strikes to demand union rates for doing construction work. But support for the war effort was largely unstinting. By January 1942 Camberwell War Savings Committee was able to announce that it had raised £5,000 to buy a Spitfire, which would be dubbed *Camberwell Beauty*. Church congregations shared each other's buildings when their own were damaged or else met in the homes of parishioners. Father Potter later reminisced that "within one mile radius of the Friary [on Linden Grove in Nunhead] only eight places of worship out of twenty-six standing before the war, could be used." Among major churches totally destroyed by enemy action were St Matthew, Denmark Hill, Camden Church, Peckham Road, St Mary Magdalene's, St Mary's Road, Peckham and St Clement's, Friern Road.

After the ending of hostilities a number of A.R.P. posts formed social clubs to perpetuate wartime comradeship. And in Dulwich alone four local heroes were awarded the George Medal for rescuing casualties from bombed-out homes at risk of their own lives. The total of civilian deaths in the borough ran to 1,014, of whom 29 were Civil Defence personnel. The number of injured was 5,742.

In the wider conflict Camberwell men and women also naturally played their part. The First Surrey Rifles became an anti-aircraft battalion and in the 1944 battle for Caen in Normandy, Corporal Sydney Bates, son of a Camberwell rag and bone man, persevered, despite three wounds, with an attack which forced an enemy retreat but cost him his life. Awarded a posthumous V.C., he was buried in the War Cemetery at Bayeux under the inscription "His parents proudly remember him as a true Camberwell boy and a loving son."

Pioneering Initiatives

The spirit of Dr Lettsom, like some therapeutic *genius locii*, appears to have lingered into the present century, during which the local community has benefited from a series of pioneering projects in social welfare, housing and public health.

EDWARDIAN ENTERPRISES

At the beginning of the present century severe physical disability condemned many to lives of institutional dependency for lack of suitable occupations and accommodation. In 1912 Alice Blanche founded her Home for Invalid Women Workers in Love Walk. Here the inmates could find a place both to live and work after receiving a training in fine needlework.

The Maudsley Hospital, erected in 1914, was named for the eminent psychiatrist Henry Maudsley, a professor at University College, London, who himself contributed £30,000 towards its foundation. The scale of this personal munificence can be judged from the fact that the annual salary for a Member of Parliament at that time was £400. A pioneer in the treatment of mental and neurological illness, the Maudsley has been responsible for training most of Britain's leading practitioners in the field of psychiatry.

BETWEEN THE WARS

Men returning from the trenches after 1918 were promised 'Homes for Heroes' by a government which, once it calculated the costs involved, backed away from this rash pledge. The Sunray estate at Herne Hill was one instance of its redemption. Begun in 1920 and eventually comprising 292 dwellings, it featured neat, low density cottage-style houses set along broad avenues edged with grass verges and shade trees.

Although physicians occasionally made successful blood transfusions during the nineteenth century, it was not until 1900 that blood groups were discovered in Vienna. In 1914 a Belgian surgeon discovered that sodium citrate could prevent donated blood from coagulating before use and in 1917 an American serving with Canadian forces found that glucose could be used to store blood for long periods. In 1921 Dr Percy Lane Oliver, a founder member of the Camberwell Division of the Red Cross, persuaded four fellow members to donate blood in response to an urgent request from King's College Hospital. From this isolated incident he conceived the idea of recruiting a permanent panel of volunteers willing

157. The fountain in Dulwich Village honours Dr Webster, a local practitioner for over sixty years and founder of the first British Medical Association.

to respond to crisis calls from any London hospital. At first demand was small, only 26 requests for blood being made in 1924. In 1926 Oliver moved to 210 Peckham Rye and used his personal telephone to manage his growing organisation until his landlord objected to the constant day and night activity inevitably arising from emergency requests, which by that year had reached 5,333. In 1928 Oliver moved to 5 Colyton Road where a G.L.C. plaque now commemorates his work in establishing the world's first voluntary blood donor service.

The idea of promoting positive health, rather than of responding to illness after it had developed, was the inspiration behind the Peckham Experiment organised by Dr George Scott Williamson and Dr Innes Pearse. After working together as colleagues at the Royal Free Hospital they teamed up in 1926,

158. The house overlooking Peckham Rye from which the world's first blood donor organisation was administered.

using a house in Queen's Road as their base. In 1935 they were able to move into a concrete and glass purpose-built building, appropriately named the Pioneer Health Centre, in St Mary's Road. Designed to the specifications of the physicians by the distinguished architect Sir Owen Williams, it combined the facilities of a club and a clinic, providing both regular medical checkups as well as leisure and sporting facilities. Arthur Mee's guidebook to London described the Centre enthusiastically as:

"a great club house for the families of Peckham, where they find every encouragement known to science to be healthy and happy and wise. Here they may dance, fence, play games, enjoy physical exercises and swim in a beautiful blue-green bath. There is a children's bathing pool with a playground, a library, a cafeteria, a kitchen, a hall and a running-track. In setting up this great Health Centre Peckham has set a fine example to the densely peopled areas of our great cities. The West End of London has nothing to equal it."

The programme ended in 1950, the year in which Williamson and Pearse married, both in their sixties. He died in 1953. Her account of their work, *The Quality of Life: The Peckham approach to Human Ethology*, was published a year after her death in 1978. Curiously, the Official Handbook produced by Camberwell Borough Council to mark its Golden Jubilee in 1950, omits all mention of this remarkable venture, despite devoting lengthy sections to recording half a century of improvements in local health services and standards.

159. *A scene in the Pioneer Health Centre, St Mary's Road. The building is now a campus of Southwark College.*

160. *Inside the Peckham Pioneer Centre in the early 1940s.*

Envoi

In 1950 King George VI was still on the throne and Mr Attlee still presided over a Labour government. Partial rationing remained in force. But Camberwell was *en fête,* celebrating its Golden Jubilee as a Borough. The Official Handbook that it published to mark this civic milestone was part chronicle and part programme of events; it ran to 152 pages and was sold for sixpence, just a penny more than the price of a pint of milk. The Handbook's Foreword was faced by a portrait of the Mayor, Alderman A.F. Crossman J.P., dutifully at his desk, wielding a fountain-pen and, somewhat improbably, wearing his massive chain of office. Poised at mid-century between an old world and a new one, he was shown sporting a wing-collar but flanked by two telephones.

Jubilee events were co-ordinated by the Council's Public Relations and Entertainments Committee which created for the purpose a consultative Celebrations Council, with representatives from forty-five local bodies, ranging from the Dog Kennel Hill Community Association to the Dulwich and Sydenham Hill Golf Club, and embracing the various enthusiasms of weight-lifters, allotment holders, cyclists, cricketers and model-makers.

The main schedule of events ran for over a fortnight, starting on Saturday 13 May. In the morning of that day there was the official opening of an Exhibition of Local Industries and South London History Pictures at the South London Fine Art Gallery. In the afternoon came a grand procession and pageant, which assembled at Dulwich Common and wound its way along Lordship Lane, Grove Lane, Champion Park and Denmark Hill, through Daneville Road, Camberwell Church Street and Peckham Road to reach its final destination on Peckham Rye. Participants included not only contingents from local schools, hospitals and service organisations, but also floats representing the Astoria Cinema, Old Kent Road, the Dutch Boy Laundry, the Glebe Operatic Society, the Ruskin Stables and the South London Film Society. The evening concluded with a Grand Carnival Dance at Co-operative House, Rye Lane – tickets 3s. 6d.

Events over the following two weeks included

161. *Hard times after the War: Food parcels for Christmas 1948 sent from the people of Camberwell, Australia. In November 1948 the Borough presented a Certificate of Freedom and a silver casket to Cllr W.R. Warner J.P., Mayor of Camberwell, Victoria, in recognition of his efforts in organising gifts of food during the war and its austere aftermath.*

162. *The cover of the Jubilee handbook published to mark the 50th anniversary of the Borough of Camberwell in 1950.*

evening band concerts in public parks, competitions in golf, cycling, table tennis, darts, speedway, swimming, tennis, boxing and athletics, a ball-room dancing demonstration by World Champions Bob Burgess and Margaret Baker, and a Round Camberwell Quiz chaired by B.B.C. presenter Gilbert Harding. One particularly striking feature, a Grand Variety Physical Culture Display, was arranged by the Camberwell Weight-Lifting and Body-Building Club, which was almost as old as the Borough itself, having been founded in 1907. Its Principal, the appropriately named W.S. Pullum, famed as a world-champion, was apparently able, through his links with the 'Health and Strength League', to organise a weight-lifting contest with contestants from the 1948 London Olympics, plus 'The Four Georgians – Hand-Balancing par Excellence" and a Judo "Ably – and amusingly – demonstrated ... Including '*Lady versus Bandit*' feature." The serious business of local government was itself incorporated into the festivities. On Tuesday 23 May the new Denmark Hill Housing Estate was officially opened and the following day at the Annual Meeting of the Borough Council the election of the Mayor took place.

Further events were organised throughout the summer. In June, Rotary Clubs and the South London Press Flower Lovers' League combined efforts to organise window-box and garden competitions – including the judging of cultivated 'Bombed Sites'. In August, to occupy children during the school holidays, there was a special youth programme, with festivals of drama, music and literature, demonstrations of physical training and dancing, and a cricket match against a West Indies XI.

Although the Official Handbook expressed the cautiously optimistic hope that "The good work done during the Jubilee Year might well be continued in future years to the advantage of all inhabitants", the Dulwich *Villager* concluded sadly that "it is no secret that from the point of view of public interest, the recent Camberwell Jubilee was a failure. On the surface it would appear that in this Borough there is little sense of community consciousness ...". Perhaps this was a harsh judgment. When the last tram ran through Camberwell a couple of years later there was a tremendous turnout to witness its passing...

163. *Camberwell greets its last tram in 1952.*

Chronology

967 First recorded mention of Dulwich.

1086 Camberwell and Peckham surveyed in Domesday Book.

1127 Dulwich granted by Henry I to Bermondsey Abbey.

1152 St Giles' parish church rebuilt in stone.

1275 Two women brewsters recorded at Camberwell.

1279 Gilbert de Clare, Earl of Gloucester, Lord of the Manor of Camberwell claims the Assize of Bread and Ale (i.e. the right to fix prices).

1290 Name of the vicar of St Giles', Camberwell recorded for the first time.

1544 Manor of Dulwich granted to the Calton family.

1550 John Bowyer marries Elizabeth Draper, acquiring the manor of Camberwell Friern.

1558 St Giles' register of baptisms, marriages and burials begins.

1603 Plague kills over a hundred parishioners.

1605 Manor of Dulwich sold to Edward Alleyn.

1615 Wilson's Grammar School founded.

1616 Christ's chapel, Dulwich consecrated.

1619 Edward Alleyn founds his College of God's Gift.

1625 Second major outbreak of plague.

1626 Death of Edward Alleyn.

1657 Congregational chapel opens in Meeting House Lane, Peckham.

1665 Great Plague carries off more than one hundred parishioners.

1674 Camberwell Vestry established.

1706 Greencoat School founded.

1721 New Greencoat School building completed.

1727 Camberwell workhouse established.

1739 Friern Manor map drawn

1741 James Allen's Girls School founded. De Crespigny family move to Champion Lodge.

1745 Brewhouse recorded at 37 Peckham Road.

1748 First recorded sighting of Camberwell Beauty butterfly.
Grove House Tavern built.
Camberwell Hall built.

1767 Bell House, College Road built for Alderman Thos. Wright.

1776 Act of Parliament authorises lighting and foot patrol for Camberwell.

1779 J.C. Lettsom buys Upper Springfield estate.

1782 Turnpike road extended from the Elephant & Castle to Camberwell Green.

1785 Belair built for John Willes.

1787 Act of Parliament authorises lighting and foot patrol for Peckham.

1789 Dulwich turnpike gate established.

1797 Camden Church, Peckham Road opened.

1798 Camberwell Military Association established under the command of Claude Champion de Crespigny, with Dr Lettsom as Medical Officer

1801 Population of Camberwell parish 7,059. Construction of Grand Surrey Canal begins.

1802 Part of Dulwich Common enclosed.

1804 Glenlea, Dulwich Common built for Charles Druce.
William Claude Champion De Crespigney entertains the Prince of Wales.

1810 J.C. Lettsom sells Grove Hill mansion.

1811 Surrey Canal completed from Rotherhithe to Camberwell Road.

1812 Robert Browning born at Rainbow Cottage, Cottage Green.

1813-14 St Chrysostom's, Peckham Hill Street built as Peckham Chapel.

1815 New workhouse opened in Havil Street.

1818 Camberwell New Road opened.

1819 Grove Chapel built.

1821 Friendly Female Asylum opens in Chumleigh Street.
Mrs Elizabeth Coade dies at Camberwell Grove.

1822-4 St George's church built.

1823 Ruskin family move to 28 Herne Hill.

1825 Denmark Place Baptist church built.

1826 Surrey Canal branch to Peckham completed.
Peckham House opens as a mental asylum.
Elementary school established at St George's church.

1827 Peckham Fair abolished.
First Vestry Hall established.

1829 Metropolitan Police established.
South Metropolitan Gas Company established.

1831-2 Cholera outbreak – 107 deaths in Camberwell parish

1834 Camberwell Collegiate School for Boys established.

1835 Poor Law Guardians established in Camberwell.

1837 Denmark Hill Grammar School established.
Aged Pilgrims' Asylum established .

1838 Bethel Asylum established.

1840 Nunhead Cemetery opened.
Pelican House girls school opens in Dr. Lettsom's villa.

1841 Population 39,868.
St Giles' parish church burns down.
Champion Lodge demolished.
1841-2 Emmanuel Church, Camberwell Road built.
1844 Rebuilt St Giles' parish church opens.
1842 Gas first installed in private houses in Camberwell.
1845 Camberwell appoints first District Surveyor.
Champion Hill Residents' Association formed.
1846 Camberwell House opens as a mental asylum.
1848 St Matthew, Denmark Hill built.
1849 Cholera outbreak – 504 deaths in Camberwell parish
1851 Thomas Tilling inaugurates horse-bus service from Peckham to the West End.
1852 Lambeth Building Society established.
1853 Father Redcap rebuilt.
1854 Crystal Palace is moved to Sydenham.
Camberwell Burial board established.
Cholera outbreak – 55 deaths in Camberwell.
1855 Camberwell Fair abolished.
Metropolis Management Act reforms Camberwell Vestry, conferring powers over sewerage, drainage, paving, cleansing and lighting.
Acorn Wharf established on the Surrey Canal.
Zion Methodist Church, Neate Street opened.
1856 Camberwell Old Cemetery opened.
1857 Camberwell Green saved from speculative development.
Dulwich College Act passed.
1858 G.E. Street remodels St Paul's church, Herne Hill.
1859 First Surrey Rifles established.
1860 First Roman Catholic church opened in Camberwell.
1861 Population 71,488.
Bowyer House demolished.
1862 Railways reach Camberwell.
1863 Flora Gardens, Wyndham Road are built over.
Sir Henry Bessemer buys estate in North Dulwich.
1863-5 St John the Evangelist, Goose Green built.
1864 London main drainage system reaches Camberwell.
1864-5 Queen's Road Wesleyan Methodist church, Peckham built .
1865 Camberwell Vestry assumes responsibility for former turnpike roads.
Volunteers' HQ opens in Flodden Road.

1866 Last cholera outbreak – 46 deaths in Camberwell.
Denmark Hill Station opens.
1867 Jones & Higgins opens in Rye Lane.
1868 East Dulwich (then Champion Hill) station opened.
Samuel Jones 'Butterfly' brand stationery factory established.
1869 Magistrates' licence required for premises selling beer and cider.
1871 London School Board established.
Double-decker horse tram service begins between Elephant & Castle and Camberwell Green.
1872-3 New Vestry Hall built.
1873-4 Barry Road Methodist church built.
1876 Catholic Apostolic church built.
Mary Datchelor School established.
Roller-skating rink opens.
1877 Board Schools opened at Comber Grove and Albany Road.
1878-1880 Peak of building activity in Camberwell – 416 firms or individual builders erect 5,670 homes.
1880 South London Baptist Tabernacle established.
1882 Act of Parliament establishes separate Boards for the administration of Dulwich College Estates and the Foundation Schools.
Wilson's Grammar School rebuilt.
1884 Princess Frederica opens public hall in Rye Lane.
1884-5 St Clement's, Friern Road built.
1885 Trinity College Mission founded.
1886 James Allen's Girls' School reopens in East Dulwich Grove.
1887 Albany Chapel demolished.
1888 Nunhead FC established.
1889 London County Council established.
Cambridge House Settlement established.
1890 Dulwich Park opened.
1891 Population 235,344.
Calvary Temple built.
South London Fine Art Gallery opened.
1892 Camberwell Baths and Dulwich Baths opened.
1892-1905 Gas-meters installed in working-class housing.
1893 Camberwell Central Library opens.
Dulwich Hamlet FC founded.
Cambridge House Settlement founds Hollington Boys' Club.
1894 Peckham Rye park opened.

1895 Peckham Rye Tabernacle established.

1896 Oriental Palace, Denmark Hill opens (renamed Camberwell Palace 1899).
Nunhead Library opens.
Demolition of Half Moon Hotel, Herne Hill.

1898 Crown Theatre Peckham opens.
Camberwell School of Arts & Crafts opens.
Demolition of The Greyhound, Dulwich.

1900 London Government Act establishes Metropolitan Borough of Camberwell.

1901 Population 259,339.

1903 Electric tram service inaugurated.
L.C.C. assumes educational responsibilities from London School Board.

1905 North Camberwell Baths opened.
One Tree Hill opened as a public space.

1908 Northampton House demolished.
Tram service extended to Peckham Rye and Dulwich.

1910 Peabody Estate built at Camberwell Green.

1909-13 King's College Hospital built.

1912 Centre for the Disabled established at Love Walk.
New Grand Hall Cinematograph Theatre opens in Camberwell New Road.

1914 Maudsley Hospital opens.
Gladys Cooper opens Tower cinema.

1916 Camberwell New Road station closes.

1917 Zeppelin raid kills 22.

1920 Building begins on Sunray Estate, Herne Hill.

1926 Pioneer Health Centre established in St Mary's Road.

1927 Camberwell New Cemetery opened.

1929 William Booth Memorial College opened.

1931 Dr Harold Moody founds the League of Coloured Peoples at 164 Queen's Road, Peckham.

1934 Camberwell Town Hall remodelled.

1935 Royal visit to Camberwell marks Silver Jubilee of George V.

1936 Crystal Palace burns down.

1937 Metropole Theatre/Camberwell Empire demolished.

1939 Camberwell Empire replaced by Odeon cinema.

1944 Bombing of Dulwich College and Dulwich Picture Gallery.

1948 Cambridge House opens Britain's first adventure playground on a bomb-site in Camberwell.

1949 Ruskin's house at Denmark Hill demolished.

1950 Camberwell Borough celebrates its Golden Jubilee.
First phase of Burgess Park opened as North Camberwell Open Space.

1951 Peckham House closes as a mental asylum.

1952 Electric tram service ceases.

1953 Sacred Heart Roman Catholic Church opens in Camberwell New Road.

1954 *Kentish Drovers* public house, Peckham demolished.

1955 Camberwell House closes as a mental asylum.

1956 Tower cinema closes.
Camberwell Palace closes.

1961 Camberwell Samaritans established.

1963 Demolition of St Chrysostom's, Peckham Hill Street.
Catholic Apostolic Church converted to become St Mary's Greek Orthodox Cathedral.
Cambridge House establishes an adult literacy scheme.

1964 Day centre for single homeless opened in the crypt of St Giles.

1965 Metropolitan Borough of Camberwell abolished.

1967 Lugard Road dairy closes.

1969 Magistrates Court opened at Camberwell Green.

1970 The Camberwell Society established.
Grand Surrey Canal filled in.

1971 The Rosemary Branch demolished.

1975 Wilson's Grammar School moves to Sutton.

1980 Jones & Higgins, Rye Lane closes.

1982 Selborne Estate opened.

1985 Butterfly Walk Shopping Centre opened.

1992 St Barnabas' Church, Dulwich destroyed by fire.

1993 St George's Church, Wells Way converted to flats.

1994 St Michael's, Wyndham Road becomes London's first Anglican church with a woman vicar.
Camberwell Green Health Centre opened.
Odeon cinema replaced by the Foyer centre for young homeless.

1996 Re-dedication of St Barnabas' Church, Dulwich.

Further Reading

D.H. ALLPORT: *Collections Illustrative of the Geology, History, Antiquities and Associations of Camberwell and The Neighbourhood* (1841)

D.H. ALLPORT: *A Short History of Wilson's Grammar School* (revised edn 1964)

JOHN D. BEASLEY: *The Story of Peckham* (London Borough of Southwark, 1983)

JOHN D. BEASLEY: *Who was Who in Peckham* (Chener Books, 1985)

A.R. BENNETT: *London and Londoners in the Eighteen-Fifties and Sixties* (T. Fisher Unwin, 1924)

W. H. BLANCH: *Ye Parish of Camerwell: A Brief Account of the Parish of Camberwell Its History and Antiquities* (E.W. Allen, 1875; reprinted by the Camberwell Society 1976)

MARY BOAST: *The Story of Camberwell* (London Borough of Southwark, 1996)

MARY BOAST: *The Story of Dulwich* (London Borough of Southwark, 1990)

G. BRODRIBB: *Felix on the Bat* (Eyre & Spottiswoode, 1962)

CAMBERWELL BOROUGH COUNCIL: *Camberwell Golden Jubilee: Official Souvenir Handbook* (Ed. J. Burrow & Co. Ltd, 1950)

ARTHUR R. CHANDLER: *Alleyn's: The First Century* (Charles Skilton, 1983)

TIM CHARLESWORTH: *The Architecture of Peckham* (Chener Books, 1988)

E.T. COOK: *Homes and Haunts of John Ruskin* (Allen & Co., 1912)

HUNTER DAVIES: A Walk round London's Parks (Hamish Hamilton, 1983)

J.S. DEARDEN (ed.): *The Professor: Arthur Severn's Memoir of John Ruskin* (George Allen & Unwin, 1967)

J.S. DEARDEN: *John Ruskin's Camberwell* (Brentham Press, 1990)

H.J. DYOS: *Victorian Suburb: a study of the growth of Camberwell* (Leicester U.P., 1961)

BRIAN GREEN: *Dulwich: The Home Front 1939-1945* (The Dulwich Society, 1995)

BRIAN GREEN: *Dulwich Village* (Village Books, 1983)

SHEILA HODGES: *God's Gift* (Heinemann 1981)

STEPHEN HUMPHREYS: *Britain in Old Photographs: Camberwell, Dulwich & Peckham* (Sutton Publishing, 1996)

TERRY NORMAN: *The hell they called High Wood: the Somme 1916* (Stephens, 1984)

DAVID A. VAUGHAN: *Negro victory: the life story of Dr Harold Moody* (1950)

OLIVE M. WALKER: *A Tour of Camberwell* (H.H. Greaves, 1954)

RON WOOLLACOTT: *A Historical Tour of Nunhead & Peckham Rye* (Maureen & Ron Woollacott, 1995)

INDEX
Asterisks denote illustrations